Praise for *The Fc*

It takes a poet to understand the depth of beauty of the Mass because the Mass is itself a profoundly beautiful poem. Every word, every gesture, every movement of priest and server are charged with the grandeur of God. The Mass moves in rhythm with the beating of the Sacred Heart. Fr. Michael Rennier understands this. He understands the poetry of the Mass, musing on its mysteries. This is not merely another book about the liturgy. It is a song of praise.

—*Joseph Pearce, Author,* Literary Giants, Literary Catholics *and* Faith of Our Fathers: A History of True England

Fr. Rennier asks: "When you go to Mass, listen closely. Do you hear the heartbeat of Mother Church?" If not, you will after reading *The Forgotten Language: How Recovering the Poetics of the Mass Will Change Our Lives.* This book brims over with beautiful imagery and abounds in powerful metaphor. It addresses sublime issues, yet in a down-to-earth, intensely personal, and oftentimes humorous way—a most enjoyable way to grow deeper in our love for God through the truth, beauty, and goodness of the Mass.

—*Kevin Vost, Author,* Memorize the Faith! *and* You Are That Temple!

Fr. Michael Rennier makes a passionate case for giving the best of ourselves and of the wonder of creation back to God in regular, ordered worship where the details matter. He shows how, through beautiful liturgy, we can enter into that dance of giving, receiving, and "grace-filled rest" that is the inner life of love shared by the Trinity.

—*Katy Carl, Author,* As Earth Without Water *and* Praying the Great O Antiphons: My Soul Magnifies the Lord

"Are we today really hopelessly huddled in our own little circle?" asked Ratzinger in his *The Spirit of the Liturgy*. "Is it not important, precisely today, to pray with the whole of creation?" Rennier's poetics of the Mass, premised upon his own reversal from huddled comfort to stripped-bare soul, teaches us what humble and humbling grandeurs such a prayer would unveil, what luminous pitches and secret dramas become palpable when we dwell poetically at the hinge of Heaven and earth.

Collapsing tired and false dichotomies—of "dead external forms" vs. "authentic worship," of "artsy intellectuals" vs. "ordinary believers"—this thoughtful poetics of the Mass reaches through aesthetics to grasp the exquisite hem of God's own garment. Here is a vulnerable and heartfelt homage to the healing power of the Holy Sacrifice—an ordered eruption of overpowering grace that lowers self-important postures onto liberating knees, and converts the contortions of ego into a cruciform awe. Rennier reveals the Mass as measure of everyone and everything else: by attuning us to its meter, its rhythms, the heart of its art, he sets down a wager: do we wish to assert our own petty preferences—to be weighed and found wanting—or lifted up into the music of God, which is one long verse, our one long laud? But it is the Mass's punctuations of perfect silence, more than Rilke's mute "Archaic Torso of Apollo," that whisper, without ceasing: "You must change your life."

—*Joshua Hren, Co-founder of the MFA at the University of St. Thomas, Houston, founder of Wiseblood books, author of* Contemplative Realism: A Theological-Aesthetical Manifesto

The Forgotten Language

The Rev. Michael Rennier

The Forgotten Language

How Recovering the Poetics
of the Mass Will Change Our Lives

SOPHIA INSTITUTE PRESS
Manchester, New Hampshire

Sophia Institute Press
Box 5284, Manchester, NH 03108
1-800-888-9344
www.SophiaInstitute.com

Sophia Institute Press is a registered trademark of Sophia Institute.

paperback ISBN 978-1-64413-658-4

ebook ISBN 978-1-64413-659-1

Library of Congress Control Number: 2023931079

For Amber, if ever I've managed to make anything beautiful, it has been with you and for you.

Contents

The Forgotten Language

ONE

In the Beginning

WHAT DOES IT mean to be a creature made? To not exist at one moment and then, with the crack of a rib broken, be spoken to life, poured from the heart of the Creator to stretch your mud-flaked arms and legs, open your eyes to peer, wide-eyed. Before you know it, you're toddling along the couches and coffee table, blurting out words in some secret language all your own, fishing for worms in puddles after a rainstorm, tracing the veins of a maple leaf with your finger, lying in soft green turf, wondering, dreaming, luxuriating in the cool touch of clayed earth, crying out to your mother to please, please look at the harvest moon because it's like a giant glowing lamp.

Frustratingly, in the matter of describing your own existence, who you are, what it means to be made, how to situate yourself in such a bright and beautiful world, you are tongue-tied.

These are questions of what we call *poetics*. What does it mean to be made? What does it mean to be a maker? "Poetics," says Igor Stravinsky, "is the study of work to be done." Although related to poetry and art, which are things made and incarnations of creativity, poetics is a more universal concept, one that concerns us all.

Poetics isn't limited to the talent of a select few artistic geniuses. We are all made in the image of the Creator God who has made the cosmos and calls it good. Part of what it means to be human is to be creative, to reflect God's beauty back to Him. This work, this making, is for everyone.

Poetics is the art of living. For a Christian, it's also the art of learning to live as a saint, an exploration of what it means to claim that God is remaking us through grace.

The questions are simple, really. How do we live? What does it mean to die to self and become saints? How to live beautiful lives, meaningful lives that are living poems?

The answers, such as they are, reveal surprising depths because they excavate the heart of our human experience and our relationship with God. To be perfectly honest, there's no complete answer. At best we gesture toward the truth which can only be worked out with fear and trembling in the midst of a living, breathing human life.

The picture is muddied by our innate conception of pilgrimage as a straight line, as if we leave the past behind once we step into the future. In fact, the past is always with us. Sainthood isn't the abandonment of who we once were, but the abandonment of sin — that which kept us from being what we're meant to be, and thus the redemption of who we once were. Further, it's the promise of what we are to become. At every moment, we are departing and arriving.

The advent of Christ into creation as a human person, and further, into baptized hearts, is revolutionary. By showing up, He reaffirms His creative commitment. He walks among us as an artist yet. He's still writing the story. Baptism is, to be sure, a death to self and resurrection to a new man. We hold to this truth while at the same agreeing with G. K. Chesterton when he points out that a revolution is, by definition, a circling round. This is why Stravinsky says, "Art is by essence constructive."

Grace doesn't destroy what came before. Grace is poetic revolution, a circling back for the sake of transformation. In the beginning, chaos is identified with the void. Creativity is contrary to this chaos. Sin and mediocrity are identified with it.

Now, here's where it gets personal, because sin, chaos, and the temptation of comfortable mediocrity are the story of my life. I dare say that many of you have some similar story. What follows in the rest of this book is a poetic confession, the meditation of a man moving uncertainly from chaos toward beauty. It's an analysis of what it means to have been made by God and what type of making, or work, He places in our hands. It all began with the Mass.

My personal experience is not your own, but we hold in common the fact of our creation and ongoing recreation by God's grace. This places upon us the vocation to be creative ourselves, for we are made in His image.

This is the challenge. It isn't to be taken lightly. Our task, our poetic and, we might even say, priestly task, is to connect earth to Heaven.

This work cannot be undertaken apart from its source, the Holy Sacrifice of the Mass. The Mass is where our High Priest, Jesus Christ, accomplishes His most beautiful, most creative work.

✠ ✠ ✠

In the beginning, like a seed buried in warm dark earth, is the *Logos*. The *Logos* is related to logic or divine reason, but more than anything, He's the Word. Our Lord isn't an idea or a logical puzzle to be solved. He is the Word spoken from all of eternity into the void.

God is not distant. He desires to communicate so we might know Him, really know Him. In order to do this, He assumes human flesh and speaks.

Having been made in His image, we, too, have the capacity for speech — talking, listening, thinking, forming ideas, letting our imagination run wild, making music, and so on. Our words, if they're good and beautiful, speak into the void, participating in the Word that encompasses all other words. We're children who begin to speak exactly how we hear our parents speak.

The purest form of language is poetic. Poetry is the most attentive, careful, and meaningful type of speech, capable of saying far more than would seem possible because the words point to a greater reality beyond their literal meaning. Christ Himself, as our Great High Priest who mediates for us, connects Heaven and earth in His very being, fully God and fully man, as a sort of living poem. He is pure creative act, the Word forever on the lips of the Father.

The Holy Sacrifice of the Mass is directly authored by our Lord at the Cross. It's the source and summit of our faith because it's where we sacramentally encounter Him in the flesh. It's where He acts most powerfully. The Mass is the ritual language of the Church by which she welcomes the Poem. By unifying herself to the Poem, the Church, through nuptial mystery, also becomes poem.

So, perhaps you begin to see how I've come to the conclusion that, fundamentally, our entire life is poetic in shape. And it all begins with the Mass.

Maybe that sounds too impractical, this idea of poetry and the Mass, but really, beauty is something we can all receive from God and return to Him. It's far more important and fundamental than we think. Without beauty we cannot live.

I'm not a poet. I've written some verse but it's what might charitably be described as "pedestrian." I still write poetry only because I have so much I desperately want to say. As I told my mother when she asked if I had enough thoughts to fill an entire book, "Oh, goodness, yes. I could write a million books." There's so much I want to say. I'm not sure if this is healthy, this entitlement to blurt out my innermost thoughts as if they're so very important. (I strongly suspect if I actually wrote a million books, the vast majority wouldn't be worth reading.) The expectation that you will find me fascinating is, perhaps, audacious to the point of verging on our old enemy—yours and mine: the sin of pride.

On the other hand, we all desire to communicate and make a genuine connection. When I read a good poem, I feel I've become friends with the author. Right there on the page, through the magic of language, a soul is laid bare and my own reaches out to meet it. I've often thought that, if we could really, truly communicate exactly what we feel, if we could capture the expansive reality of what it means to be alive—write a perfect poem, for instance, something like "The Windhover" by Gerard Manley Hopkins—there's no reader in the world who wouldn't find it so winsome that a friendship wouldn't immediately be formed. To know another person with perfect accuracy would make it difficult to also not perfectly love them. Maybe that's why our Lord, who knows us inside and out, loves us so.

It's the same feeling, I imagine, as a memory I have of being a teenager and talking to my girlfriend Amber—now my wife of twenty years—on the telephone. Lying on the floor as night fell heavy outside the windows, we talked about nothing much in particular. Laughing, I revealed my best, most closely guarded secrets. Those conversations reduced the cosmos in size—or expanded us in size—until it was only us two. It was perfect communication, a language that birthed unbreakable love.

Poetry is like spilling your guts to your childhood sweetheart. It's a miracle that anyone ever manages to write it, to dig so deeply into the meaning and structure of language as to unveil some vital aspect of Being. Writing a poem seems more difficult than cramming the sun into a box to keep on my nightstand.

Poetry has a reputation for being impossible to understand, a literary exercise in arrogance for dreamy intellectuals. I don't believe that. Not for a moment. Poetry is eminently practical. Far more than a few words, it opens up a new door in our experience of existence.

Throwing caution to the wind, I relentlessly quote poems to parishioners during homilies. I'm sure they're tired of it. I'm sure they gently poke fun, though they never complain. My parishioners are an indulgent lot. In their patience, I sense their love. They love Jesus, love the Church, love the Mass, and love their priests. As a spiritual father who barely knows what he's doing, I try my hardest to love them back. Mass just wouldn't be the same without them. As Cardinal Newman once joked, even if the relationship between priests and laity is sometimes strained, we priests would look pretty silly without you all. A poem is nothing without both author and reader.

Understanding the Mass as poetic is challenging, yes, quite challenging. Poetry is more difficult to read than prose. Entire books are filled with analysis of even short poems, but everything of value is difficult. Repeating clichés and commonplaces is easy, because it substitutes for real communication. Real communication requires vulnerability. Any words can take on a poetic character if they're honest and beautiful, open and generous, at service to the wonder and fragility of human existence.

Perhaps the real reason poetry is considered difficult is that it requires love. Love is difficult. To those audacious enough to attempt it, love can be harsh and demanding. It exacts a price. Love is most fully expressed at the Cross. At the heart, it's self-sacrifice that takes everything away for the sake of another.

We can all live poetically, which is simply another way of saying that we all participate in the divine love that pours itself into every creature. It's a love that overflows and pools like deep water. Like St. Peter when he discerned the Risen Lord, I encourage you to jump in with both feet. Who really cares where the bottom is — there might not be one.

The Mass is a love poem, an ocean with no floor. It cannot be contained. Unbounded, it clings like incense, gets inside us, and reshapes our souls to make them ever so much larger. The more love fills us up, the more our souls expand, until it becomes strikingly clear there is no possible human explanation for how all that love fits in the world. It's an impossibility of grace, a paradox by which a finite heart holds an infinite and edgeless love.

The great mystery of our lives lies in following that poetic thread, holding on for dear life while it guides our pilgrim steps toward the vast, awful, unnameable reality to which the poem gestures and in which it participates.

The Mass is the perfection of the Church's poetic skill, the divine Artist's stanzas laid bare to read, page after page of a letter written from one lover to another. It's high time we read with the attention it deserves.

What does it mean to experience the Mass as poem? It changed my life.

This is the story of how that poem transformed me: how I began, through missteps and self-inflicted wounds, to live poetically, allowing Christ to Word every moment with beauty. It's the story of how the Mass can change you, too.

TWO

Like a Moth to a Candle

BEFORE ANY JOURNEY can begin, the destination must be known. The Mass is both the journey and the destination, the way to Heaven and simultaneously a participation in Heaven itself. It's the treasure map and the treasure. The problem is, in our sinfulness and confusion, we so often follow a different map, and the prize at the end of the rainbow, whatever shiny toy we were chasing, is moth-eaten and rusted. We look in the wrong places.

Before even a single word is spoken at the Mass, the sacred architecture of the church shows us where to look. Ideally, the Mass doesn't take place in just any old room. It takes place in a church. The way the space is shaped in a church building is important to understanding how the Mass is all about our conversion into new creatures.

The journey mapped out at the beginning of the Mass is that of the Israelites leaving Egypt. The journey the Israelites undertook is also the story of our Faith. We are with them every step of the way.

The first thing you'll see in many churches, just inside the doors, is the baptismal font—it's shaped like a womb. You dip your fingers and bless yourself with the holy water. Like the Israelites leaving Egypt, you are symbolically leaving the captivity of sin behind, crossing through the baptism of the Red Sea and into freedom. The very first words in the book of Exodus are about lineage and fruitfulness. It's a story about the rebirth of a nation. Moses himself is reborn from water when he's rescued from his papyrus basket that was floating in the Nile. The Israelites are reborn when they process through the Red Sea. We are reborn when we are baptized.

Past the baptismal font, you take your place in the pew. Soon, the sacristy bell rings and the opening procession begins down the center aisle, led by a server swinging a thurible billowing with incense. This places us in the footsteps of the Israelites as they follow the pillar of smoke. The candles the altar boys hold represent the fire they follow by night.

The procession finally crosses through the altar rail that divides the nave from the sanctuary. The sanctuary is the Promised Land, which in turn is a metaphor for Heaven. The food for the journey is the unleavened bread the Israelites stuffed in their pockets as they hurried from Egypt. Later, in the desert, they are fed with manna. In the Mass, the Eucharist is brought down from the sanctuary and dispensed to the faithful, who have come up from the pews and stopped right at the threshold between the sanctuary and the nave. There, the faithful receive Christ. As a people we are still, in terms of sacred architecture, in the desert. Christ comes down from the altar like manna from Heaven to feed us.

The space itself — the architecture, the procession — it's an imaginative poetic description of the wilderness, a place of testing and preparation. This spiritual desert is where you and I face our temptations. The Mass is where Christ tabernacles with us and joins in the struggle. Over the course of our lives, we either turn away from Him and perish in the desert to be buried in the sand with our sins, or we approach the altar, receive Christ, and allow Him to recreate us. He and He alone will lead us into the Promised Land.

✠ ✠ ✠

Each year, I throw myself into the wilderness. Well, not the wilderness precisely. Rather, a country house situated on family property tucked into a wine-producing valley along the Missouri River.

The point is, I'm alone for a full week. I possess a melancholic personality, and being solitary for too long is a recipe for overbaked ruminations on mortality and the long loneliness of seeking perfect love in a world that seldom cares much about you or me. I end up splayed out on the dock down by the pond, staring at buzzards circling updrafts and greedily eyeing how much meat clings to my bones. If our Lord went into the wilderness for forty days to battle Satan, and Moses led the Israelites into the desert for forty years to contend for the Promised Land, after a mere forty hours I'm a quivering fish gasping for air, shimmering. Flopping.

To me, during these retreats, the rolling oak-covered hills the Missouri carves through on her fickle path become a daunting wilderness, in turn staggeringly beautiful or a savage lion's den. I feverishly write poems in an attempt to come to terms with the sadness of being away from my children, a sadness which opens up the frightening realization that they will grow up and leave home anyway. I cannot be home to all the people and places I love, and I'm a permanent traveler entrusting my most precious experiences to memory before leaving them behind. Each day must be lived generously with an open hand, as life streams through our fingers like sand.

This wild and unpredictable creation, containing all manner of people and beauty and joy, is so lovely it aches. It's overwhelming. Astonishing beyond belief. Selfishly, I want to grab and hold on, wrapping myself with beauty forever. I picture myself like Our Lady of Guadalupe wrapped in a mantle of stars. I absurdly envy Dorian Gray, who managed to stall time even at great personal cost. Beauty, though, is a flying bird, and the more tightly we grasp, the faster it takes wing and slips over the horizon.

You and I are on a journey to God. We seek the silent, still place at the center of a vast whirlwind where all the distractions, anxieties, and doubts drop away and we finally, truly rest. Leaving behind the thin footing of this limited world that cracks like ice under footfall, we are on our way. Out and past the hedgerow of Eden, we cannot stand still. We must keep moving, ideally with the burden of a cross. Even if, when we pause to look back, every place we once loved has changed.

These are the overwrought, nostalgic thoughts to which I'm prone while on retreat. A simple, unassuming spiritual retreat, to be clear, is literally all I'm drawling about. As a Catholic priest, you would think I'd be more accomplished at spiritual development, but every sighed prayer, every sustained attempt at contemplation, every woebegone effort to practice silence in the presence of the Almighty feels like the most difficult undertaking in the history of mankind. Every other day, I distract myself with parish business, errands, thoughts to think, people to chat with, cups of coffee that must be brewed and savored, homilies that must be written and must be profound. On my spiritual retreat, alone, those defenses are thrown down. I must pay attention to the state of my soul. I must pay attention to God. In the process, I fall to pieces.

The problem, as I see it, is that I'm hopelessly incapable of paying sustained attention to anything that really matters. It's astonishing how quickly I become confused about what's important, and how slow my soul is to bend toward it. I desire easy pleasures, easy entertainment, comfort, spiritual candy. I'll gladly toss my cross away for a television show, or gossip, or to check sports scores on my phone. I focus on career goals, what to eat for dinner, and I crunch numbers to see how long until we pay down the house mortgage.

In the parish, I like to estimate Mass attendance and count up the number of newly registered parishioners. It's truly pointless. I look in all the wrong directions.

Where am I looking? What's worthy of being looked at? Gerard Manley Hopkins, the priest-poet, confides to his journal, "What you look hard at seems to look hard at you."

✠ ✠ ✠

I grew up in a religious culture that emphasized personal, emotive experience. My parents gifted me with a living faith, for which I'm grateful. I went to church from a young age, at St. Louis Family Church. There, flags of every nation hang from the ceiling, under which are row after row of chairs. The chairs are comfortable—comfortable enough, Pastor Jeff would joke, for a three-hour-long service. We all laughed and clapped, but he wasn't actually joking.

Church became the center of my existence. My friends were there, and my social life and spiritual life were there. Every Sunday, we settled in for long sermons that closely hewed to the Scriptures. I even took notes, scribbling into the margins in my Bible. Others were doing the same. The world can be a harsh place. It can and will starve a person, mentally and spiritually. We were there to be fed and restored. We hung on every word. The way we pored over the Scriptures, we may as well have brought magnifying glasses.

We attended weekly prayer meetings, pacing the perimeter of the room, kneeling, sometimes sitting together in silence before the Lord. Waiting. There was a collective anticipation. What would He say? With the trust of little children, the kind of trust bestowed only by faith, we waited.

I wanted to hear from God, to know where my life was heading. I gravitated like a moth to the nearest light. My church friends were going to Oral Roberts University, so I went to Oral Roberts

University. I formed a desire to become a pastor. I was hesitant but resolved to explore the idea.

Oral Roberts is a campus that sparkles like a rhinestone. Oral, a televangelist, tent-revival preacher, built the university in a style he thought looked impressive. It was a testament proving that the particular flavor of the gospel for which he was an ambassador had finally achieved respectability. Gold covered the buildings, including a space needle at the heart of campus. Just off campus is a skyscraper of sixty stories. It erupts out of the suburban architecture of south Tulsa. This, to Oral, was the architecture of the future. Many floors in the skyscraper, to this day, remain unfinished.

When I arrived, the campus hadn't aged well. Oral had retired and disappeared to a mansion in California, and the steps to the main classroom building were falling to pieces. One of the two eternal flames — one eternal flame wasn't enough — had been permanently switched off. The flame was supposed to burn until Christ returns in glory.

Richard Roberts ran the university after his father left. He was an aspiring lounge singer who deployed his showbiz charm on church audiences. Once a year, the students were required to attend a live taping of his miracle-healing show. He would hold his hand out and instruct the television audience to touch their hands to his on the screen. Southern gospel music played while the miracle happened.

It was around this time that I stopped going to church.

If God was calling me to be a pastor, I was going to be a lousy one. That much was clear. Once I became serious enough to pay attention, I became cynical and bitter about what I saw in the local Pentecostal churches, which I thought were populated by manipulative pastors getting rich off of gullible audiences. Intellectually, emotionally, and spiritually, I was quickly becoming a mess. I was a dying star ready to explode. Icarus with melting wing.

Looking to salvage my faith, I became fascinated by Catholicism. I began calling priests in Tulsa and asking them to defend the doctrine of transubstantiation. I went to their rectories and demanded defenses of Catholic beliefs. They gave me cheap coffee and listened as I ranted about crooked faith-healers. They showed me their parishes and asked about my background.

One of my professors, Jim Shelton, was a Catholic deacon. He gave me the documents of Vatican II. He probably doesn't know this, but I actually read them and was impressed. Conversion, however, isn't only intellectual. The intellect is necessary, for sure, but faith is a gift. In retrospect, I was already halfway into the Church but not ready to surrender. I was angry because I suspected the Church would conquer me, but I couldn't admit it yet.

What we cannot say out loud remains but an unformed idea. It has power and meaning proper to an idea, but left unworded, it languishes. It would take a real encounter with God to finally shake me free from my egocentric, noisy search for the truth and take notice, to understand where all those departures into all those wildernesses were leading. I was being led, steadily, to the Mass.

✠ ✠ ✠

The first Mass I attended, I was eight years old, taken by my Catholic grandparents to St. Joseph's. I was greatly impressed by the repetition of kneeling and standing inside the old country church, which was warmly painted and accented with stained glass and brightly colored statues of saints. Those saints were gaudy mysteries, nameless, serious, pious wonderworkers, ambassadors of a Faith somehow related to but quite foreign from mine. I knelt and watched a single-file line of worshipers have the bread placed in their hands. I wondered what sort of test one must pass in order to be included. After Mass, a series of kindly old people—old to me, at least—warmly greeted me and my brothers.

We were the grandchildren of Carl and Elaine. My grandparents were fixtures in the community. In fact, at the Mass we attended my grandmother was the reader. She went up onto the stage and got to read into a microphone. I thought she was a very important person indeed.

The second time I attended was a decade later, at Holy Family Cathedral in Tulsa. Older now, in college, I was still innocently ignorant, spiritually laden with Bible Belt Evangelicalism. This second time, I looked right and left before gingerly sliding into the pew, burdened with all manner of preconceptions, theological commitments I'd developed in theology class and instilled by latching onto various one-liner insights gleaned from the homilies of local Pentecostal pastors. The mysteries and symbols of Catholic devotion were awkwardly lit by the light of my own, skewed narrative. I left disappointed and confused. I couldn't admit it, but even though I was put off, I also desperately wanted to go back again. I was afraid one of my classmates would see me, though.

The third time I went to Mass was on summer break from college. In St. Louis, there's an old German parish, St. Francis de Sales, built by immigrants in south city but since given by the diocese into the care of the Institute of Christ the King Sovereign Priest. It rises above the row houses, a monument to the power of popular devotion in better days. It was—and in some ways still is—crumbling to the ground, the bell tower threatening to splay out across the parked cars and power lines and lay down on Gravois Road. When given to the Institute by Archbishop Burke, the parish was dying, empty and cavernous on Sunday mornings. The stained glass windows were melting out of their frames, and the suffocating summer humidity of St. Louis was peeling the plaster from the bones of the structure. Nevertheless, the building is an architectural treasure, a neo-Gothic house of worship with a soaring interior. The Institute has rescued the parish and it has become internationally famous.

I'd been told by a friend that it would be like time-traveling to the medieval ages—a full, Solemn Latin Mass with Gregorian chant. I was impressed I wasn't the only one to wear a jacket and bow tie in the sweltering heat, and even the numerous children present had a certain dignity about them. As the little ones fussed, their mothers calmly knelt and prayed, the teen girls wore lace veils, and the teen boys served in the sanctuary. The priests went about their work, the chant drifted from the loft, and God appeared on the altar.

God sank His arrow. This third time Christ looked me full in the face and asked if I loved Him. He gently but insistently asked me to throw plans and comforts aside to feed His sheep. I was but a tumbling lamb myself, racing to God knows where, but the arrow pierced skin and flesh. Mortally wounded by beauty, I was unmade.

God's unmaking is an unveiling. I saw it there in the Holy Sacrifice. The Poem. A candle in midmost midnight, illuminating a fresher, more dear, more deep-down reality I might inhabit by accepting that nail-punctured hand. An invitation to death. The invitation to truly be alive.

✠ ✠ ✠

So much of our lives, we don't pay attention to the right things. We become distracted by career, gossip, anxiety, and our own indulgences. I worry about how my hair looks, how my 401k balance is faring, what my wife is going to make for dinner. It's all so insubstantial, but when we're in the midst of it nothing seems more important.

What's fascinating about the Mass is that it doesn't even pretend to fit in with life-as-usual. The liturgy creates its own culture. It plays by its own rules. Almost as if it's trying to jar us loose from our tired, battered sensibilities, by immersing us in a completely foreign experience. It's a way of poetically shouting, *look over here, feel this sacred ground under your feet, breathe this strange atmosphere, timeless and wide.*

When Simone Weil discovered the Mass at the monastery of Solesmes, she fixed her mind like a trap upon its loveliness, particularly the sung prayer of the monks. The chant was so different than anything she'd heard before. It made her stop and listen.

When I went to that Mass at St. Francis de Sales, I was baffled from the start. The chant was very beautiful, but very unfamiliar. The vestments on the priest and deacons were antique emerald-green silk damask. Each sacred minister wore a biretta with a blue pom on top. They were preceded in procession by about thirty seriously devout altar boys attired in matching blue cassocks. It was obvious that we were being drawn into a culture created for another world. This wasn't a liturgy meant to fit in with the things of earth. It was meant to transform the earth entirely.

When the sacred ministers passed through the altar rail, they moved up to the steps at the foot of the altar and there, while the Introit drifted down from the choir loft, they paused. They stood there. I could see they were saying something among themselves, but it was inaudible. I felt their hesitation. The overlapping of realities. The sense that we were being confronted by the full majesty of Almighty God and that the sacred ministers weren't quite sure how to react.

Later, I learned they were praying the Prayers at the Foot of the Altar. The heart of the prayers is Psalm 42,[1] the *Judica me Deus*, after which they pray the *Confiteor*. It's such an odd juxtaposition of prayers. The Psalm declares, "Vindicate me, O God, and defend my cause against an ungodly people." And then the *Confiteor* chimes

---

[1] According to the numbering of the Vulgate, the translation of the Bible used in the Latin Mass.

in with a prayer of penitence: "I confess, to Almighty God ... that I have greatly sinned." The first declares innocence and the second confesses iniquity. Here, right at the beginning of the Mass, the priest is stopped in his tracks before the mysteries of God's love, a love strong enough to encompass both justice and mercy.

If there's a rule that governs the Mass, it can only be that the humble will be exalted. How else can the iniquitous be declared innocent? How else can we look upon God, receive Him on our lips, and live?

It was only later that I learned the content of the Prayers at the Foot of the Altar, though. That first time I witnessed them, I only knew that the priest was being very careful. He didn't do what I expected him to do, which was march up to the altar and begin speaking. That hesitating preparation was like a divine finger pointing to the altar where a precious secret was about to be unveiled.

✠ ✠ ✠

After my initial encounters with the Mass, I would stumble out the church door, having been coughed up like Jonah from the whale. As Herman Melville writes of his own symbolic whale, stabbed from behind with the thought of annihilation and simultaneously beholding the white depths of the Milky Way. I was at a loss.

This is very much what the poetic accomplishes. It leaves us staggered, gasping for air, not because it suffocates but because it's taking in breath from an entirely different atmosphere, a whispered message saturated with oxygen, so rich that you feel your heart will burst into flame. Leaving those Catholic churches and driving home, I tried to process the experience.

"What have I been missing all my life?" I wondered.

✠ ✠ ✠

God tells Ezekiel, "O mortal, eat what is offered to you; eat this scroll" (Ezek. 3:1). He eats, calling it sweet as honey. Full of divine poetry, Ezekiel is carried on the wings of angels. He hears the sound of wheels turning and knows he's going to be ground under them like wheat in a mill. "I came to the exiles," he says, "I sat there among them, stunned, for seven days" (Ezek. 3:15).

I suppose that's how I felt when I attended Mass as a seeker—like a stunned exile. At Oral Roberts, during free time between classes and shifts as a waiter at IHOP, I went to Holy Family. I sat in the last pew, imitating what others were doing. I'd never made the Sign of the Cross, and even that simple action, which for a "cradle Catholic" is second nature, was a poignant experience, exciting and transgressive. I'd been raised to reject ritual. A good Christian, as the lesson went, prays with the heart, not superstitious gestures. And yet, when I furtively made the Sign, I felt the presence of the saints drifting off my arm.

That simple gesture disarmed me, and I dropped all my preconceptions. Everything was different than what I'd supposed. I noticed actions, gestures, and words that seemed to have deep meaning of which I was ignorant.

Today, as a priest, I hear people ask why we don't cut the pageantry at Mass and simplify. Vestments, singing, incense, statues, bells, holy water—it's all, strictly speaking, unnecessary. Sure, we could cut the prayers to a few sentences and save time, but the Mass wouldn't be the Mass anymore. We would have changed it into a grace-dispensing machine or an intellectual exercise. It's so much more. It's real, the Word become flesh.

Ezekiel describes the gratuitous extras in painstaking detail. How many reeds high the wall around the Temple is; how thick the wall is; the size of the vestibule and gateway; how the pilasters are carved with images of palm trees. He walks the outer court pavements, measuring every chamber, corner, and niche. He examines the altars where offerings are slaughtered and burnt. Eventually, he is led into the Holy of Holies. He measures it, a perfect cube, twenty cubits square. He retreats, still measuring and describing every detail, writing, "Each cherub had two faces: a human face turned toward the palm tree on the one side, and the face of a young lion turned toward the palm tree on the other side. They were carved on the whole temple all around" (Ezek. 41:18–19).

Only after Ezekiel has paid close attention to the house of God and its worthiness does he turn to look over the horizon, writing, "And there, the glory of the God of Israel was coming from the east; the sound was like the sound of mighty waters; and the earth shone with his glory" (Ezek. 43:2–3). God speaks, "As for you, mortal, describe the temple to the house of Israel, and let them measure the pattern" (Ezek. 43:10).

After this follows detail upon detail about the Temple and the worship that would take place there. Only after proper attention has been paid is Ezekiel shown the river flowing from under the altar. A river that grows in power and strength. It feeds the land and makes it fruitful, growing deeper and deeper until it cannot be crossed by human strength alone.

God cares about the details, each one a building block creating the form in which the water of life is contained. It's poetry in action.

✠ ✠ ✠

I'm currently a married Catholic priest, ordained under the pastoral provision created by Pope St. John Paul II for former Anglican clergy. My wife Amber and I have six children who have taught me the value of paying attention to the poetic shape of our lives. To my toddler, a generic tree is an object worthy of lingering over: a sap-scarred oak, triumphant against an ancient wind, strong as a king yet kind enough to gently drop a gift for her, a single trembling leaf. She carries it home in one hand while allowing me to hold her other hand in mine. As we walk, her pockets jingle with stones she has collected and saved.

I've missed so much in my need to talk and fuss, my arrogance and busyness. Now I make up for lost time. With my children, I look at airplanes in the sky. We look at mommy ducks and baby ducks, bird nests stuffed with mottled blue eggs, and fish flopping and shaking off drops of emerald-green water before we release them with a triumphant cry back into the lake. I love it all.

Love sharpens our vision. The lover sees most true. I'm grateful to my children for revealing that creation is wildly rampant with God's love, that it is gratuitously flung from His hand, shattering into shards of diamond. He is waiting for me and you, His little children, to look, to notice the sparkle under our feet and stoop to investigate.

If creation so generously rewards those who look closely with child-like attention, how much more so will the Mass? Here, in the sacred liturgy, if we look with great love, we will behold not only some *thing* that is lovely, but some *one*. We will not only have an experience of beauty, but a transcendent encounter with beauty Himself.

In my experience, participating in the Mass is hard. It takes effort and concentration. There are days we don't want to be there or are distracted by worries, but Beauty is always there, right there at the altar, waiting for us to notice.

✠ ✠ ✠

When I celebrate Mass at Epiphany of Our Lord, where I'm the pastor, and I manage to pay attention, this is what I notice:

In the sanctuary, the morning sun arrives through stained glass in the eastern side of the apse. The white light divides like a prism, sending colored beams to the tile floor in a jeweled pattern. The sun is warm on my face, but the coolness of the night lingers in the stones of the century-old building. The church is an ancient body warmed from within. Dust motes play in the air over the colored squares. Most of the world is still asleep, but I'm here. I mark out my days by walking rounds in the silent church, praying the Daily Office, preparing for Mass.

Outside, the faint sound of cars. Workers to the office, children to school. Inside, I'm waiting. The door gently swings open and closed as the faithful gather. The shift of knees on the dry, cracked leather kneelers. A sigh. The click of a rosary bead. Outside, the crocuses lift their faces to the sky. Inside, the brass candlesticks on the altar glimmer. The wind moves slowly across the clay roof tiles. Clouds are passing. The Host almost afloat on my fingertips. The bell in the tower lazily rolls. Time is spilling out in whispered prayers. I've fallen down a sacred well where my voice echoes but gently returns like waves to the shore. The sunbeams slip the prism. Everything is bright and transparent. We're in a clear stream and sunlight plays off the pebbles in a thousand directions. I see far. Very far. A draught carries extra oxygen to the candle flames. There's infinite horizon yet to be crossed, but it doesn't frighten me, only brings contentment and the indescribable feeling that this place, this time, consumed by this sacred action, is where I belong. It's where I fit. The cassocks of the altar boys rustle in unison. A kneeler falls from a hand to the floor with a bang. We are held in a strong hand, strong enough to crack the world apart, but it doesn't because it is very kind. It has no need of proving its power. The thurible chain bends onto itself with a sound like a waterfall. I make a Sign of the Cross, look at the crucifix, and bow over the altar to consume the Host.

✠ ✠ ✠

Attention is love. It burns me up inside because there's one place that, in my ego, I like to focus, and that is on *myself*. It's a road to nowhere, leading only to despair. The world is an occasion of temptation and confusion; all too often we cannot identify the right choices because the situation before us is muddled. Our gaze is captured by temptations and distractions. We fall back on our own resources and look inward, which pulls us down like a stone dropped from a hand.

It's an act of love to look away from ourselves. It's a sacrifice, a spiritual death and a constant departure into the wilderness. I struggle with this calling out from myself to pay attention to God. I don't believe God holds anything back from us—after all, He is our Daily Bread, but I fail to take and eat. The universe, my destiny, the heart of God—they're written in a language of which I sense the meaning but cannot quite translate.

When I was experiencing the Mass as a non-Catholic, I had a dawning appreciation for attention. I wanted to grow young, like a child, and watch with wide-eyed innocence. It was difficult because I was still on the outside. I hadn't yet discovered how vast the interior of the Mass truly is, how it ascends word by word, rung by rung on a ladder to Heaven.

Funny thing is, by the end of my annual retreats, which are so personally challenging, I feel amazing, like I've ascended a mountain and done battle with dragons. I often have the same feeling after Mass. If, on your spiritual journey, you've found yourself wrestling with beauty, hesitant before the poetic mystery of the Mass, you might find that God has touched you on the hip and you're limping. That's good. It means you've sought. You've looked. You've grabbed hold and have been touched by God.

THREE
Named in Silence

OUR FIRST CHILD, a daughter, was born on Cape Cod in winter. In the pale pre-dawn we drove to the hospital in Hyannis. Snowflakes swirled in the headlights and melted on the windshield. She arrived a few hours later, squishy faced and astonished, into a world whose walls aren't wide enough to contain her.

Almost in shock, all I remember is the bustle of nurses, the horror when I thought they were going to make me cut the umbilical cord, an inky foot, and a blank birth certificate put into my nervous hands. It dawned on me that I was expected to take the pen and write into the blank space the name of my daughter. I watched her sleep. Her toes stretched. She hiccupped. Her eyes flickered back and forth behind closed lids.

Choosing a name is a sacred responsibility. I honestly don't know how babies manage to get themselves named. But named they are, and everyone seems to be walking around, meeting new people and casually tossing out their name by way of greeting. At conferences and meetings, they write their names with permanent marker onto disposable name tags like it's no big deal. Maybe even dotting the I with a heart or writing a smiley face next to it. Somehow those names, every one, are fitting to each person. To call them by any other word seems absurd. It's a miracle.

✠ ✠ ✠

> So out of the ground the Lord God formed every animal of the field and every bird of the air, and brought them to the man to see what he would call them; and whatever the man called every living creature, that was its name. (Gen. 2:19)

I wonder if Adam trembled when God brought him those anonymous animals. How do you come up with a descriptive name for a tiny flying bug that unfurls painted wings as delicate as tissue paper? *Monarch butterfly.* Is the name enough to encompass the reality of the creature? The way it migrates in boreal orange clouds, north to south, across a continent that pushes from sea to sea, and arrives to the same exact tree it has called home the year prior? Where it then flowers forth on a gentle breeze with its paper wings, mounting up to a sound like a cascading stream, as powerful as the movement of the angels themselves through our fragile atmosphere? This creature, its manner of being itself, is indescribable. Words are not enough, as anyone can agree who has stood on a mountain peak, swum in the ocean, watched a child play, or even watched the sun melt into the roof of the neighboring, suburban house. You have to be there.

Yet, there is poor Adam, a general before his troops as they march past in full uniform on the parade grounds. Evaluating, defining, naming. Perhaps trembling.

It makes sense that the higher creature would name the lower. There's a reason we name the animals but the name of God is unknowable. Still, the Scriptures slyly allude to Adam's unease with the whole endeavor. Among all the creatures there isn't a single one with whom he fully connects. Their souls are hidden and, even as he prodigally flings out names, silence springs up between them.

In response, God puts Adam to sleep and opens a wound. From that wounded heart he creates Eve. The two are bound by the wound, which is a symbol of mutual sacrifice, the cost that love and poetry and beauty require. Even as a piece of himself is taken away, Adam remains in a deep sleep, a death-like state. Eve arrives in silence.

Love is a roofless sky, a voiceless house. What Adam and Eve share cannot be named. There are silences that are empty and silences that are full.

The reality of who my children are, the way they've pried open my heart—this cannot be named. I've given them my best attempt at good and beautiful names. I researched long and hard, thought and prayed. I presented my list of ideas to Amber like a sacred scroll, but even so, what these kids even now are becoming breaks all boundaries.

Over time, though, a strange phenomenon occurs with names. They begin to fit. The word expands and acquires a history all its own. It summons forth the interior reality. I call for my child and, lo, my child appears. I cannot imagine calling them anything else, but that's not because the name contains them. They contain the name.

Every person is a living poem authored by God, and everything worth saying is in the blank spaces between the words.

✠ ✠ ✠

The procession at the beginning of the Mass leads the eye forward and focuses us on our journey to Heaven by way of the sacrifice of the Cross, but the space itself also physically rises upwards. The great gothic cathedrals were meant to rise up to Heaven, like stone flowers turning their faces to the sun. Through the use of line and form, they insist on drawing the eye upward, often toward massive, colored windows. The space is flooded with light and the atmosphere feels alive, providing at the same time a feeling of home and celestial striving. There's something about the air itself that poetically shapes our experience of worship. It's as if we're meant to look up to the sky and keep looking until we're firmly in Heaven.

The sky signifies that the universe is vast but also glows with divine love. Poets have written about the sky from the very first Homeric hymns the Greeks composed. In them, the sun is made sacred as Helios, the god who drives a golden chariot shepherded, as Pindar puts it, by fire-darting steeds.

There are days the sky is stretched tight in seamless blue and spills through the windows of the Church during Mass, and I feel I'm falling upwards along with the Host. We could be lifted away in an instant, so near is our Lord.

Christians have always been sky-watchers, from following the star to the nursery of Christ to keeping our faces turned east so we might be the first to greet Him when he returns like the rising sun. In the ancient Church, the altar always faced east for this very reason, to watch for the Second Coming. This is why, for instance, St. John writes in his Apocalypse that an angel comes up from the east. The angel is arriving from Heaven.

In sacred art, the view behind our Lord is typically the western sky. At the Last Supper, for instance. Remember, it's the first Mass, and Christians always celebrated *ad orientem*, with people and priest looking together to the east. This means that, if we're seeing the face of Christ at the Last Supper, He's looking east, so we're across the altar looking west. In paintings of the Ascension, we are again looking west because we see our Lord's face as He rises toward the east. At the Cross, too, we look west because the good thief is always to his right, on the south which represents the brightness of the New Covenant. This insistence in sacred art on the western sky can only mean one thing—Catholic art shows the view from Heaven, from the east, from the perspective of the rising sun. The events are depicted as seen from eternity, the viewpoint of a saint. All of this we intuit, without a word, simply by looking at the sky.

Each day, no matter how busy, I pause for a moment and look up. Everything goes quiet. No anxieties, no schedule, no clock, no breaking news, no gossip. I can almost hear Hopkins shout, "Look at the stars! look, look up at the skies! O look at all the fire-folk sitting in the air!" He's adamant that we stop and look. The fire-folk Hopkins is looking at are stars, which his imagination turns into the communion of saints floating like luminaries in the sky.

As seen through Catholic art, the sky is an inversion, taking us from the perspective of earth and placing us into the perspective of Heaven. From here we see reality the way the saints see it. It's an inversion:

> Blessed are the poor in spirit....
> Blessed are those who mourn....
> Blessed are the meek. (Matt. 5:3–5)

We might even say that, from God's perspective, everything is upside down. What we thought was of first importance is actually last. It's enough to make anyone speechless.

While exiled on the island of Patmos, St. John sees the sky unroll and Heaven unveiled, an event that simultaneously happens at the end of time and also right now within the Mass. Christ is revealed in both. At Mass, we look ahead to the day when we take our place in the communion of saints, but also when we take our place in the communion right now.

I imagine St. John sitting at the beach after sundown, the sand still radiating the warmth of the day past. The stars rotate across the sky and he dreams of the heavenly throne room. He sees our Blessed

Mother at the side of Christ and knows that she is his mother, too. Perhaps he keeps vigil over the eastern waters, toward Jerusalem his lost home, and thinks of the Church, his friends and family left behind, martyred or scattered to the ends of the earth. The stars dangle like saints standing vigil and, in an inversion worthy of the Beatitudes, peace descends, the assurance that we, the Body of Christ, cannot be riven — not by time, distance, or death.

Under the sky, in the presence of the saints, at the Mass, we don't have to speak because we are being spoken to. It's all poetry, an inversion of what we thought we knew. We don't earn our place in the communion — we receive it. We are gathered like golden wheat to the barn. We are looking east, toward our salvation, lit by the language of hope. The priest holds the Host in his hands, lifted high, the rising Sun. Look and see what love the Father has bestowed upon us.

✠ ✠ ✠

I've never been a loud person. No one would describe me as boisterous, extroverted, or animated. In my own way, though, I create my fair share of noise. As a college student searching for answers, I was particularly fond of useless debate, cynical back-and-forths aimed toward cleverness and rhetorical point-scoring. I loved to bask in the sound of my own voice. I used to think arguing was fun. It's so embarrassing.

I thought God owed me some answers. Like a toddler demanding a chocolate ice cream cone with sprinkles, I asked the same questions over and over. I told Him to justify Himself, explain to me why I wasn't happy, why I stayed up all night in dread of the morning, why every nerve I had was stretched thin as razor wire over cut glass. I was reading, debating, complaining, objecting, analyzing. I thought it was a sincere spiritual search, but it was all noise.

Dr. Shelton suggested that I visit an Episcopal church down the street, the Church of the Holy Spirit. I thought it would be a nice change of pace from my usual habit of absolutely refusing to go to any church at all, so I told Amber I would like to try it.

The first difference we noted in Church of the Holy Spirit from a typical Pentecostal church was an absence. In Pentecostal churches, there's no conception that a space might be sacred, so people freely mingle and chat. However, when we entered this Episcopal church, there was almost no noise. The atmosphere was expectant. A few children whispered. There were brief, murmured greetings in hushed tones as people took their places in the pews. And that was it. We had entered a room containing several hundred people kneeling before God in silence. It almost made me cry.

✠ ✠ ✠

Before Eve is drawn from his side, Adam must sleep. At the making of his covenant with God, Abraham falls into a sleep of terror. Only then does a floating flame make its bloody passage carved from the corpses of sacrificial animals. When Christ dies, creation groans and then blackens in silent mourning. His body is tended to in horrified silence and sealed up in the grave. In St. John's Apocalypse, the Lamb opens the seventh seal and silence reigns for half an hour. After naming my daughter, I held her without a word.

Everything important is covered in silence.

There's an ancient homily for Holy Saturday, the day our Lord is in the grave:

Today there is a great silence over the earth, a great silence, and stillness, a great silence because the King sleeps; the earth was in terror and was still, because God slept in the flesh and raised up those who were sleeping from the ages. God has died in the flesh, and the underworld has trembled.

Christ approaches Adam:

I command you: Awake, sleeper ... I slept on the cross and a sword pierced my side, for you, who slept in paradise and brought forth Eve from your side. My side healed the pain of your side; my sleep will release you from your sleep in Hades.

It makes me wonder, do we realize what is birthed in the silence of the Mass?

✠ ✠ ✠

Poems are oddly fragile. If broken down to a fundamental level, we discover silence. Obviously, a poem forms words. It communicates or it is nothing. This is a paradox of the poetic form. Only out of silence does God speak. Hovering over the womb of the void, He creates. It's through deep sleep, the silence of both the womb and the grave, that language, transfigured, arises.

Poetry creates silence through attentive, careful use of language. Each word, bearing multiple levels of meaning, is chosen by the author and set in place. Each one rubs up against the word next to it, causing friction and casting a spark that glimmers just outside our field of vision. If we turn to look directly at it, it disappears. We only achieve a sideways glance. Its meaning is precious. It lights our path and feeds the soul, but we never capture the light source.

To confront reality without any filter—well, that's a frightening prospect. The face of God is lightning and earthquakes. We really have no idea how He hides the fullness of His presence under the shadow of mere bread and wine, fits into a human heart, or soundlessly words our existence. It's an encounter in which we cannot conquer. We can only surrender.

This is what it's like to read a poem. Silence cradles the words, and only those who listen carefully notice this and receive the gift. In the Mass, too, the ancient poetry arises out of silence and returns to silence. The priest must be reverent and gentle, devoted to an *ars celebrandi* which is a form of silence all its own. He must not add his own words to those of Christ the Eternal High Priest. He must not be noisy. A poem is far more than words, and the silence of the Mass is far more than we suppose. Practice silence and receive the gift.

An ecologist named Gordon Hempton has been sitting in forests for decades, listening. He nestles into mossy redwood roots and waits. He isn't seeking a means of escape. Rather, he's making a connection. "Silence is not the absence of something," he says, "but the presence of everything."

For thousands of years, monks have known this secret. *Into Great Silence*, a documentary about the Carthusians of the Grande Chartreuse Monastery in the French Alps, barely has dialogue, only a few lines over the length of a three-hour film. The monks serenely work—stirring a pot of porridge, shoveling snow out of the garden to prepare for spring planting, ringing the chapel bell to call the men to prayer. Their only words are to sing the Divine Office and pray the Mass. As I watched, I grew uncomfortable. I needed the monks to say something, anything, make small talk, flip on a radio, hum. I fidgeted. I paused the film and came back to it later. Still, it was silence.

I resolved to join the silence as best I could. It became the tangible presence of love. The monks are in love with God. His presence permeates their every action—distilling alcohol, sewing a robe for a new postulant, cutting celery for soup—Christ is there. Their lives are a unified whole. They don't string together a schedule—wake up, get ready, go to work, then errands, relaxation, bed—for the monks, every action is part of every other action. It's all prayer.

St. Bruno, their founder, envisioned a place of refuge from a storm-tossed world. He tells the monks, "Rejoice that you have reached a safe and tranquil anchorage in that inner harbour which many desire to reach and many make efforts to reach yet never attain." God's Word has overcome them, quenching the constant need to chatter. Instead, they listen. They are sailing over dark waters and into the Promised Land.

What most interested me when I watched the film was how the Mass seemed to arise organically from their everyday existence. Many years later, I realized I had it backwards. It was their lives that had arisen from the silence of the Mass.

✠ ✠ ✠

Elijah, stripped to the bone, quivers like a flag against the wind. Recently, he exposed the false god Baal on Mount Carmel when God rained down fire on His altar. Queen Jezebel retaliated by declaring him a dead man walking. Elijah has fled to a cave, alone, wondering if his ramshackle existence has finally come to an end. In this broken condition, God compels him, "Go out and stand on the mountain before the Lord, for the Lord is about to pass by" (1 Kings 19:11). He stands at the mouth of the dank cave, eager to feel wind upon his face, which blows so strong when it arrives that it opens up fissures in the rock. The earth shakes. A fire sweeps across the landscape. Finally, silence. He wraps his face in his mantle before God's unsounded depths.

When we really, truly listen, we hear God. When we complain we cannot hear Him, it's because we're not actually listening. Refusing to calm the noise in our heads, we maintain a ceaseless inner monologue and carry it around like an anchor. Distractions, the things we tell ourselves are so important, are nothing more than schemes to avoid reality. Cardinal Robert Sarah, in *The Power of Silence*, says, "Our world no longer hears God because it is constantly speaking, at a devastating speed and volume, in order to say nothing."

Sin is a form of noise that's highly effective at drowning out God. Cardinal Sarah describes the noise of our ego, "which never stops claiming its rights, plunging us into an excessive preoccupation with ourselves." He goes on to catalog other kinds of noise: "The noise of our memory, which draws us toward the past . . . the noise of temptations or of [spiritual sloth], the spirit of gluttony, lust, avarice, anger, sadness, vanity, pride — in short: everything that makes up the spiritual combat that man must wage every day. In order to silence these parasitical noises, in order to consume everything in the sweet flame of the Holy Spirit, silence is the supreme antidote." We're always in a battle to halt the noise.

Gordon Hempton says what he likes most about silence "is that, when I listen, I disappear. I disappear."

Elijah leaves a footprint in the dust. A terebinth raises quietly, quietly its face to the sky. In the fading cries of the pagan priests, the breaking of day, the violence that ebbed, broke, and ran down the mountainside, he is left with a valediction. God was there before. He is there after. The prophet hears the unfamiliar Name only in the after, only standing unprotected, alone and quiet.

We listen because we love. I listen to my friends even if I'm not interested or am dying to speak on my own topic, because I love my friends. I listen to my toddler tell excruciatingly long, disjointed narratives of her day because I love her. Our Lord withdraws alone to listen because He loves His Heavenly Father. I pause and listen to the wings of migrating geese overhead because I love every single day of life I'm privileged to experience on this beautiful earth.

Listening is a form of desire. I desire to hear God and I'm convinced that, if I am very still and very attentive, I'll hear His voice echoing off the clouds, rising up from springs and rivers and through the suspiration of the pines and wild Missouri grasses. As Hopkins, too, reassures himself, "Thirst's all-in-all in all a world of wet."

At Mass, be very still and very quiet. Try it because you love God. Do you hear water rumbling from the broken rock?

✠ ✠ ✠

After visiting Church of the Holy Spirit, I fell in love with the Book of Common Prayer, which guides the liturgical practices of the Episcopal Church and the wider Anglican Communion. The Book of Common Prayer is pure poetry. Chesterton put it well:

> The Book of Common Prayer is the masterpiece of Protestantism. It is more so than the work of Milton. It is the one positive possession and attraction; the one magnet and talisman for people even outside the Anglican Church, as are the great Gothic cathedrals for those outside the Catholic Church. I can speak, I think, for many other converts when I say that the only thing that can produce any sort of nostalgia or romantic regret, any shadow of homesickness in one who has in truth come home, is the rhythm of Cranmer's prose.

I found in the BCP a new way of praying which, it turns out, I desperately needed. I was doing a lot of talking and complaining but precious little listening.

At times, I sensed a need for quiet. I would sit in the university gardens with a book, sneak into the music school and play one of the practice pianos, or sit in the chapel in the middle of the night. It was never enough.

I wasn't disciplined and was only fleetingly self-aware. Discovering the spaciousness of the Episcopal Church at prayer was a revelation. After that first Sunday, we went back regularly. Finally, here was prayer that wasn't noisy and emotionally manipulative, that had form and beauty. Soon, we registered as church members and joined a small group, and I put in my application to Yale Divinity School. I wanted to be an ordained Episcopal priest.

We made silent retreats. They weren't long, only a few days, but I literally couldn't handle them. I was desperate to talk. My head hurt from spending time with my thoughts, which swirled and raced. I couldn't calm down because, the instant I did, I was left alone, and being alone with myself wasn't pleasant. Too much sin. Too many embarrassments to ruminate upon. Too much emotional and spiritual baggage I wasn't ready to confront.

God was preparing me. He wanted to give me more of Himself, but I first needed to create space. I found the process painful—I still do—because the best arena for grace is the wilderness. If everything in our relation to God is paradox, if in our natural thinking we do indeed have life backwards and true knowledge and self-possession is a sort of withdrawal, a setting aside of self for the sake of love, this means we all have a lot of dying to do. At the Cross, presence and absence overlap.

As Wallace Stevens says of poetry, "The lion sleeps in the sun. / Its nose is on its paws. / It can kill a man." The poetics of the Mass are pure beauty. It cannot be tamed.

There are two kinds of deaths. The eternal death of the soul is marked by noise and ego. It's the abyss of self. The death caused by love is marked by humility and silence. It's the abyss of the Cross. One death is permanent loss, the other is pleasing sacrifice. It's the subtle line between destruction and reconciliation.

What makes suffering beautiful, and makes human striving and sorrow redeemable, is love and love alone. I can only sacrifice what I have to give, but sacrifice I must, even if my gift is small.

To uncover our purpose, we give ourselves away, give ourselves to what we are loving. Most of all, we must consent to be consumed, to give until there's nothing left of us at all except the love. Only in such a way can the divine voice enter the human world.

My whole life, I've been learning to get out of the way. If the Mass is God's unique method of destroying and remaking the human heart, it's a unique dispensation of knowledge but, more importantly, the irruption of an overwhelming power, the greatest force, into human affairs, an intervention that clears the ground for a new and different way to build a life. Such is the manner in which the stone is rolled away from the grave. This isn't a bad description of conversion, to be transformed into a silent listener of divine whispering.

It's impossible without sacrifice.

G. K. Chesterton often received thunderous ovations when he approached the podium to begin lectures. As the applause rumbled like an earthquake, he was known to say quietly, almost as if to himself, "After the whirlwind, the still small voice."

✠ ✠ ✠

The Mass plucks us from the noise of everyday life and offers space for contemplation. Each time I step up to the altar to celebrate a Mass, I strive to listen. I remind myself to keep my personality out of it so that God's Word can emerge.

When I lock up the church building in the evening, I turn the lights off so that the only visible light is the red glow of the tabernacle candle. I listen to the poetry of the space. Every place has a poetic voice all its own. What's the sound of a church at night with silence gathered around the altar? It's the sound of a mother's arms wrapped around a child.

Cardinal Sarah calls it "the silence of the crib, the silence of Nazareth, the silence of the Cross, and the silence of the sealed tomb" — "the bottomless abyss of his … self-emptying."

God's voice transforms lives. His voice creates planets and stars, reshapes souls, and sets angels to their vocation. Consider the Carthusian monks perched on a snowy shoulder of the Alps. Each task they accomplish is done with great care, with joy, and for love of God. They have the gift of self-knowledge because they attend to His voice. It has changed their lives. God is speaking to us, too, and He will change our lives. At Mass, in the silence of our churches, in our prayer lives, in our contemplative openness to the poetic beauty of the entirety of our lives, it's time to listen.

The Mass is an iceberg. It's mostly about what lies below the surface.

Words as we typically employ them in everyday speech are used to hide what's under the waterline. We lie, gossip, brag, create narratives to fit our preconceptions. There's a proper place for small talk, joking, or bonding over unimportant matters, but if we're always speaking, we never listen. Constant speech and activity are evasive.

The Mass, just like a poem, won't let us get away with it. In the deliberate choices a poet makes about which word to use and in what order, each word gains power, or more accurately, the inherent power of the word is unveiled.

Over thousands of years, each word of the Mass has been carved out of an immense range of other choices. The prayers have crystalized into poetry of immense vitality. With God, I'm frequently speechless. I don't know what to say or how to say it. I have emotions I don't recognize. Maybe I even want to express how badly I'm struggling but feel like it's improper to address the Almighty with my petty concerns and, let's face it, entitled demands.

Silent prayer, or contemplative prayer, is always the goal as Christians because it represents the unity of our will with His. But the silence of contemplative prayer is a full silence, not a frustrated silence because we don't how to speak. It's the kind of silence that feels like sitting with your Beloved, happy to simply to be in His presence. Most typically, it follows only after a period of meditative prayer, which is prayer that employs words and images. We begin in speech and end with listening.

The problem, for me at least, is I often don't know how to start — I feel like my words are inadequate and even presumptuous. This is why the poetic shape of the Mass was such a relief when I discovered it. The Church provides the words for us. When we pray the Mass together, we pray along with the entire mystical communion. We pray with the saints, the martyrs, and the apostles. The antiphons, the Psalms, and the Lord's Prayer are the corporate prayers of the Church, and they echo the words of Christ. In fact, the entire Mass from start to finish is the prayer of Christ to the Father. When we join in with Him, we enter an intimate communication, the conversation of Father and Son. There's tremendous value simply in verbalizing these prayers together because, as poetry, they mean so much more than we can ever grasp. And sometimes, not all the time, God's grace arrives in a special way. The words melt into silent prayer, which is the very sound of God's love.

By giving us poetic words to pray, words dense with meaning and history, the Mass gives us a voice. It fashions every one of us tentative pilgrims into poets as we make the words of the Church our own.

The beating heart of the Mass are the words of our Lord, "Hoc est enim corpus meum." The priest bends low, almost clutching the altar to steady himself, and whispers each word slowly and clearly. This is poetry that moves worlds. It rearranges souls and brings about a creative miracle. The priest neither adds nor subtracts from the words; to do so would be the height of profanity. All he can do in the presence of such majestic poetry is join his priestly voice to the priestly voice of Christ. The words spring from silence, the womb of creation.

Poems are constructed against the backdrop of silence. Creation exists in the negative space, the void, gesturing beyond itself to the fulfillment of its potential, always mysteriously related to divine wholeness. A poetic manner of life eventually empties into this vast pool of meaning, back into silence, which through the beauty of the creative act has been filled with contemplative love.

Contemplation is a withdrawal. It's a vow to cease thinking of myself, as hard as that is, and regard the object of my contemplation. To me, it's like sitting on the back porch with my wife on a warm summer evening. Her head is on my shoulder as we watch the moonlight silvering the dogwood blossoms. Our children are barefoot in the grass catching fireflies and squealing with delight. We watch them play and hold onto each other without a word.

The Mass leads us more deeply back into silence than any other speech, more than any other activity or ritual of man, because it's a poem that emerges from silence to speak the single, greatest, most mysterious Word. It's the poem of which all other poetry speaks. It's the height of contemplative love. This includes all other art, all beauty, and the entirety of the imagination.

I've often thought that the Mass is a divine pause for breath, the sigh of angels ascending and descending Jacob's Ladder. Many words are said during the Mass, yes — by priest and faithful. Prayers are prayed. Scriptures are read. Our words, though, take on the very character of silence. At some point, if we treat the Mass with dignity and reverence, contemplation takes over and the words are almost unnecessary as we begin to participate in the glorious reality itself. We're drawn from profane to sacred, from sign to the thing signified, from the outer form of the Sacrament and into its inchoate inner grace. God breathes His Holy Spirit upon His people. He exhales over the void and anything becomes possible.

Dom Dysmas, one of the Carthusians at the Grande Chartreuse, says that in the darkness when the monks sing to God, "We are like children who watch the ocean for the first time."

The true beauty of a poem isn't how it begins or ends, or how much of it can be comprehended with the intellect. The beauty of a poem is how it changes us as we read. The person I was at the beginning of a poem is not the person I am by the end. The old me disappears.

☩ ☩ ☩

I'm still waging my internal war to conquer noise. In doing so, I've come up firmly against my limitations. I'm still frightened of too much silence. My mind still wanders during Mass. I still hurry and rush about, full of anxiety. It's one thing to wax eloquent about the poetics of the Mass and poems I like to read — it's another matter entirely to make one's entire life into a poem.

I've discovered over my years of priesthood that it takes courage to contend for a beautiful Mass. Satan, it seems, is intensely threatened by beauty and will go to any length to make the Mass banal and mediocre. We cannot strive for anything less, though. The Host — always and everywhere a crucified victim — embodies the mystery of life and death.

Often, I attempt to make sense of an overwhelming experience. I want to explain it, unpack it, and analyze it, but words only dull the reality. Take death, for instance. I still remember vividly how I felt at my grandfather's funeral, watching his casket carried to the grave by my father and brothers. We use the idiom "passed away" because it's immeasurably sad to face the reality that a person has died. This limitation on our time on earth, however, is part and parcel of what it means to be human. We must accurately name and embrace it even if doing so causes pain — even if the name we give is *death*.

Leon Bloy, who was constitutionally incapable of compromise, wrote an entire book to do battle with cliché. When I read it, I realized that all over the world, across centuries, the clichés I employ like some sort of suburban buddha have been uttered over and over again and shall continue to be uttered again and again. I fall back on common sayings because I'm not courageous enough to speak wisely in the midst of a moment that has become too big. Or perhaps my courage falters at the idea that it's better to say nothing at all.

I've noticed that when I quiet down and pay close attention, the words of the Mass are unsettling. No matter how many times I say them, like a poem they form a topology, a spiritual map that indicates the depths below. Each Mass becomes part of the Mass before and the Mass after. Day after day. Each morning I wake up excited that I get to offer another.

God takes us deep, right into the heart of existence. Over the years and the thousands of Masses I've celebrated, I've found that, far from becoming cliché, the poem grows in power. Christ, if we are quiet and still, brings us right up to His side, right near His heart. It's unnerving, this invitation to name and participate in a transcendent reality, but we must not flee. We must not flinch.

Notice that, in Genesis, none of the animals satisfies Adam's need for companionship. He requires another person to share his love with. Eve is drawn from a wound in his side, right there at his heart. At the Cross, that wound is recapitulated in the side of Christ, right there at His heart. We are His Bride and He the Bridegroom, in an offer of nuptial union so intimate that to accept it leaves a permanent mark on the heart. Through that gift, we are made more perfect. Through it, we come to know Christ, the Unnameable, the Word who authors all other words.

In His presence, we don't necessarily have to speak. We are invited to rest. When the Host is lifted up during the Mass, it is draped in silence. Our vocation, at that moment, is to look and love.

Elijah, remember, hearing God's whisper in the stillness, walked off that mountain and later ascended to the empyrean in a chariot of fire.

✠ ✠ ✠

My time as an Episcopalian impressed quietude upon me like a hawk to the dove. No one ever said developing virtues, as humble as our progress might be, is easy.

I entered full-time formation in seminary not knowing what it meant to practice discipline, how to order my days by prayer, or how to be quiet enough to accurately understand myself and my relation to the universe. I learned to wake up monkishly early, even in winter, and bicycle through town to the chapel where we prayed the Morning Office in community. It was a difficult habit to form, but I noticed, one week when I was sick, that I missed it desperately. Meanwhile, intelligent, ambitious classmates curbed my brashness. After a few foolish comments in class that elicited less than optimal reactions, I held my tongue to attend to my books.

At seminary, God gave me a gift. He helped me see people the way He does. I began listening carefully, even to classmates whose opinions I didn't admire. They had vastly different thoughts about God, church, and politics than I did, but I began to feel empathy. I began to really hear them, not to argue with them but because everyone deserves to be heard. I came to appreciate how unique and interesting they were. Previously, translating people into my own little narrative conceits had not only caused me to devalue them but also to entirely misread them. In this way, too, love is the key to accuracy. Those who refuse to love misunderstand so much.

I also stopped arguing with God. I hadn't been fair to Him and it was high time I took responsibility for my own flaws. These flaws revealed themselves more readily through the quietude of the liturgical disciplines I was practicing for the first time in my life. Finally, there was a form, a structure, a shape. This is the secret to a steady spiritual life and the practice of the presence of God. There must be form, otherwise it all slips away.

My spiritual life, to be clear, wasn't smooth sailing. It still isn't. But for the first time, I had a direction. I was spending more time alone in churches around town. New Haven is full of beautiful houses of worship. I particularly loved Christ Church, where a schola chanted Compline late at night and crowds of students came to hear the voices pierce the dark.

Those years entailed a letting go, both of the need to be in control and of the obsessive compulsion to make all things meaningful according to the light of my own intellect. The experience was an unveiling of pretension. The spiritual silence I was experiencing allowed me, for the first time, to examine myself honestly. It was the first step in preparing to discover the poetry of the Mass and, beyond that, the poetry of existence.

In silence, God penetrates our feelings of nothingness, and instead of relieving them, shows that He is there in the midst of them. All places are His temple, including the deserts where we engage in intense personal struggle. As St. Mark implies, Christ is present in the sand of the arena with the wild beasts.

I wasn't yet regularly attending Masses. I was intrigued but wasn't ready for Catholicism with its sinners and saints, confession boxes and martyrs, relics and miracles. I'd come a long way, though. I'd opened a door and, through the frame, glimpsed a passing silhouette.

When I stepped to the threshold, though, it was gone. Yet I was becoming confident that God's shadow falls on everything that wakes and lives, disappears around every corner, shades every wild place and green morning, His silence broken only by the echoing footfall of my search.

"Poetry," as Jacques Maritain says, "dislikes noise."

✠ ✠ ✠

T. S. Eliot lingers in a cemetery and, as he walks along the monuments, a place of endings, he intuits a beginning:

> Every poem an epitaph. And any action
> Is a step to the block, to the fire, down the sea's throat
> Or to an illegible stone: and that is where we start.
> We die with the dying:
> See, they depart, and we go with them.

The movement of time is haunting. A look over the shoulder reveals pieces of ourselves left behind, unrecoverable. Our Lord never looks back because He knows the end of the story. Throughout His life He leaves pieces of Himself behind, orienting His entire self toward that ending. His sacrifice of love upends the curse of death and gathers the shards.

Wholeness of life through death is the meaning of our existence. Take it seriously, because it's only through Christ and the Holy Sacrifice of the Mass that we can approach our end with upraised, though tearful, eyes.

A poem is a cohesive whole. Its end is present in its beginning. The words are knit into an underlying unity and form, each one explaining the previous and the next, each one a single candle. Applied to our lives, this means that nothing is lost, nothing forgotten. Every experience we have is valuable just so long as we place it into the proper context of beauty. Our suffering has meaning right alongside our joy. The one brings meaning to the other. Death brings meaning to life. Life brings meaning to death.

Eliot says that, when we circle back around, we'll know that place as if for the first time because, once again, we've been called by the beckoning voice of love. We are birthed by the voice of God and then reborn by the voice of God calling us into new creation. Finally, we are permanently called from this life by the voice of God. Always, with each whisper, He draws us closer.

The week my grandfather died, I happened to be traveling and was in a beach town in Florida. The day I heard of his death, I went to the water. The waves hit the shore, wave after wave wallowing in their wash. Like Robert Lowell, I heard the water mutter to its hurt self. The sun glinted off the glassy sand. Nearby, my children built sandcastles. They sneaked up to the waves and then, squealing, ran from the foam. At the horizon, a seabird tilted its wings. I thought of my grandfather. T. S. Eliot says that God is but "half-heard, in the stillness / Between two waves of the sea."

☩ ☩ ☩

After graduating, I was ordained and we moved up the coast to Cape Cod where I'd been invited to serve as an Anglican priest. During my time in school, the Episcopal Church had seen a sizable number of churches and parishioners depart into the newly formed Anglican Church of North America. The schism had to do with issues surrounding sex and marriage, and I ended up following the Anglicans right out of the Episcopal Church. I pastored two delightful little parishes, the Church of the Resurrection and the Church of the Good Shepherd. I loved both dearly.

Although I'm thrilled to be exactly where I am now serving as a Catholic priest in St. Louis, I grieve those lost days on Cape Cod.

Our first summer there is when our first daughter was born. She settled into this world by listening to the slower heartbeat of her mother. She would place her ear to the breast of her mother, right up against her heart, and fall asleep with a shuddering sigh as the tension drained from her body.

Gerard Manley Hopkins compares the blue sky to the mantle of our Mother Mary, writing, "I say that we are wound / With mercy round and round / As if with air." He feels her arms around him like the atmosphere. He hears her heartbeat.

Our family, perhaps like yours, has an image of our Lord's Sacred Heart hanging on the wall in our living room. Under this picture, my wife has sat in the armchair and nursed our children to sleep countless times. She's in no hurry. She patiently cradles her babe as the moonlight slants through the window. If need be, she will hold this child for eternity. In a way, she very much does hold them for eternity.

When you go to Mass, listen closely. Do you hear the heartbeat of Mother Church?

✠ ✠ ✠

I think of the names we've given our children as a calling forth, an invitation to come and make a home with us, their mother and father, sisters and brothers. I suppose that in some way, I'd always been calling each little one in from the distance, which is why these children of mine seem to arrive more and more into themselves every single day.

A poem names. It calls out to the world. It searches the heavens. We tend to see everything as an object. We use matter-of-fact language to describe surfaces and functionality, and we adhere to convention. In doing so we fail to apprehend the mystery. A poem is a different way of speaking. It calls forth hidden grace.

My children took those names and made them their own. They enlarged them, kicked open the door, and threw open the windows.

A name is just a simple word, but beneath the word is limitless depth.

In the silence of the Mass the divine poet speaks, gently and deliberately, your name.

FOUR
Bone to Flesh

THE WORD *POEM* comes into English from the Greek ποίημα. The Latin cognate is *poema*. The definition is a "made thing." In the Septuagint, the ancient Greek translation of the Old Testament, Genesis begins, "ΕΝ ἀρχῇ ἐποίησεν ὁ Θεὸς τὸν οὐρανὸν καὶ τὴν γῆν": "In the beginning, God made the Heaven and the earth." Notice the word for *made*. It's ἐποίησεν. *Epoiesen*.

In the beginning, God poemed the cosmos into existence.

St. Paul tells the Ephesians, "For we are [God's] workmanship, created in Christ Jesus for good works, which God prepared beforehand, that we should walk in them" (Eph. 2:10, RSVCE). There's that word for poem again, this time used as a noun and translated as, "workmanship," His *poiema*. We are penned into life, an artwork made by His hands.

God is clearly invested in creating, making, and fashioning. Having made us, His children, and having loved us and beholding that we are beautiful in His sight, He subsequently seems even more interested in creating anew, re-making, and transforming us. He's still authoring.

Poetry is God's creative speech. The poetic nature of our creation is a sign of His love, but it's more than that. It's His commitment to make us beautiful from the inside out. It's an infusion of grace. God doesn't love us by telling us as much. He loves us by loving us. He loves us by writing us into the story of redemption and transfiguring us into His likeness. He's an artist and we His masterpiece, art of great meaning, splendorous, a word spoken from His heart that returns to His heart.

✠ ✠ ✠

When I went to Cape Cod, it was initially to accept an offer from a small group of Anglican Christians to help build a church from scratch. I had visited several times over the previous year and come to like them very much. Even though the entire group was only fifteen people, I agreed to take the risk with them. Looking back on it, I cannot believe I was willing to take such a chance. I suppose I didn't know enough yet to understand how big of a gamble it was, so my pregnant wife and I packed up the few possessions we had, waved goodbye to New Haven, and drove north up the coast.

When you're trying to plant a church and you're the only staff member, each day is an adventure. In some ways, there wasn't much to do. There were no pre-existing commitments, no property to care for, not a whole lot of parishioners. There were days I would look at my schedule in the morning and it was entirely blank.

On the other hand, I was motivated and full of energy, so I quickly filled my time with various schemes to grow the parish. Everything had to be built from nothing. I became competent in web design, scouted out a space to rent for Sunday worship, and began hanging around with other pastors to make connections. It was a strange sort of work. At the end of each day, I wasn't always quite sure what I'd accomplished, if anything. All I knew was that I was tired.

I'd become adapted to the disciplined rhythm of seminary, the comforting schedule of morning prayer, time to read in the library, and chapel. Seminary, the way I treated it, was like living in a gothic wonderland. I'd happily meandered around town joining social clubs, trying on bow ties at J. Press, and testing out martini recipes. Each day was a constant stream of interesting theological conversation. Now, as a pastor, I'd been thrown into the wild. I immediately struggled. Even though I had plenty of time to say morning prayers and spend time with God, I rarely did. The anxiety and activity of trying to make my little church thrive was all-consuming, even as the pace of life dramatically increased. Suddenly I had job duties, a newborn baby, a house to fix, people to meet. I was trying to go fast, like a foal with hours-old legs, wobbling, buckling.

What I needed was to go slow. I was starting at the edges, in the shallows, controlling what I could by making my plans, but I needed to begin in the center, with God, in the place from which all activity and human effort derives its meaning. Our little church was writing a poem. We were making something new.

Gaston Bachelard, in his book *The Poetics of Space*, writes, "To compose a finished, well-constructed poem, the mind is obliged to make projects that prefigure it. But for a simple poetic image, there is no project; a flicker of the soul is all that is needed." To create something beautiful, to midwife a living, breathing instance of the Body of Christ into formal existence, we had to first capture that poetic spark.

Our little church, if it was to survive, needed to be fashioned in the image of Christ. To fulfill the plan He had for us, we needed more than whatever paltry projects I might be able to propose with my seminary education. The foundational cornerstone of our parish wouldn't be a program or a building. It could only be poetic, a beauty so attractive and transformative that it changed lives. In the shadow of the Transfiguration, we so often make the mistake of building shelters when what God actually wants is for us to join

Him at the top of the hill, give our lives to Him in sacrifice, and become like Him in His death so as to become like Him in glory. As a new pastor, I needed to slow my racing thoughts so that God might light a spark in His people.

A church must be an embodiment of the beautiful soul of Christ, or it is nothing.

The same goes for a poem. The same goes for a life.

✠ ✠ ✠

"The poet's relation to terms is that of maker," says Owen Barfield. "It is in this": "that we can divine the very poetic itself." In other words, when a poet writes a good line, he creates something entirely new. The words, put in a certain mysterious order, convey a meaning that has never before been known.

Living poetically is the commitment to a unique life. You cannot live my life and I cannot live yours. As a young pastor struggling to put a new church on solid footing, I often fell into envy of other pastors. I coveted their nice church buildings, Sunday attendance numbers, and financial stability. In this regard, whatever my eyes beheld, I desired. This extended also to spiritual gifts, preaching ability, and leadership qualities. I wanted it all, but none of it was mine.

We cannot flourish as lesser imitations. As Dante points out, this is like banishment from your home. "You shall find out how salt is the taste of another man's bread," he writes, "and how hard is the way up and down another man's stairs." How absurd it is, trying to sneak the lives that have been gifted to others.

If indulged, dissatisfaction gains in speed and intensity. We become ever less grateful for blessings and more frantic to possess what other people have. As the sin takes hold, it exiles us from ourselves. After years of hearing confessions, I can confidently share that we all sin in the same ways. Sin is ugly and boring. Sin makes us less ourselves, less unique.

It is the saint who is uniquely himself and set free to be happy. Saints are eccentric in all the best ways, unashamed, joyfully one-of-a-kind. Saints have a way of slowing down to hear the voice of God speaking. They don't particularly care to keep up outward appearances. Their work is interior. In fact, a saint, for all we can tell, may have stopped completely.

Stopping for contemplation leads to an inexplicable result: interior progress. There's so much we could always be doing—but don't neglect the better path, which is to sit at the feet of Christ and wait. Here, God invites us to participate in Creation, the redemption of the soul, poetic inspiration. Barfield writes, "There is really no end to the secrets hidden behind the meanings of single words." Each word arrives into being from the essential, worded nature of Christ. Each one, including you and me, unfolds out of limitless potential.

If that poem, which is the divine call to you alone, is untranslatable to others, it's still fully expressible through poetic action. This is the best way to convey meaning—a soul transformed by God's love. In this way, the life of a saint preaches more effectively than any lecture.

We all desire insight into the meaning of our lives, to understand our vocation and discover what makes us uniquely ourselves. Slow down, pay attention to the poetry happening inside your soul.

To paraphrase Oscar Wilde, we are made by the Word. The Word isn't made by us.

✠ ✠ ✠

Even as I embarked on active ministry on Cape Cod, I was depressed, anxious, self-conscious, still breaking the habit of over-reliance on intellect, and unsure. My days were constant distraction, containing, perhaps, the illusion of progress, but only really accomplishing random movement. I may as well have walked down the Mid-Cape highway with my eyes closed.

Today, there has been progress, but the struggle remains. Each morning, I put the kettle on for coffee and check my daily schedule but, before all else, pray the Daily Office and celebrate Mass. I don't know what I'd do without this familiar ritual. However, once complete, the calendar must be honored—meetings, deadlines, projects, and emails. Then, later, kids' soccer practices, a sink full of dirty dishes, maybe a television show. In the midst of all this, I sneak obsessive glances at my phone to fret over the latest rumor from Rome, rage about the latest atrocity committed by politicians, and scan news headlines describing the latest terrible thing I'm supposed to form a strongly held opinion about and share on social media. It is anesthetizing. I'm exhausted even typing out for you the myriad, thoughtless ways I waste time, let alone actually living that way, particularly when all I want is to recapture the peaceful solitude I experience during Mass.

Here's the thing, though, the Mass isn't preparation for life. It is life. It encompasses every activity of our day.

At the beginning of the Daily Office, the Church prays Psalm 95: "Come, let us sing to the Lord, and shout with joy to the Rock who saves us."[2] Here's our primary focus, spelled out at dawn—slow down, focus, prayer, liturgy. St. Benedict comments, "Nothing is to be preferred to the liturgy." We know our daily tasks, but the liturgy is the only way of ordering priorities. Formal prayer calls us to worship and, in doing so, beckons toward rediscovery of self, the opening up of interior space.

There's beauty here. So much of our lives are marked by distraction, mindless entertainment, and relentless activity, but these only

---

[2] This is the translation from the Breviary.

serve as a (not very successful) means of escape. They're alienating, causing us to act in all sorts of destructive and odd ways. The liturgy is opposite, a homing pigeon all at once certain of itself but also a leap against gravity. As Robert Lowell says, "What is home … but the flight's lost moment of fluttering terror."

The terror is present in Psalm 95, right there in the beginning. The Israelites wander, thrust into the wilderness to learn worship. Instead they turn away, overwhelmed by the trackless waste. They feel lost. Whispers spread through camp: *better the captivity of Egypt than to leave bones scattered across the sand.* They no longer notice the pillar of fire and cloud of glory. Such miracles were taken for granted long ago. They forget the rusting armor and chariots buried in the Red Sea and Sinai rattling with thunder. Everything of value has been chased from their minds. They lower their eyes in exhaustion. The song dies on their lips.

This Psalm has been with me both as an Anglican and a Catholic. Every single day it slows my pulse. Fifteen years ago in the chapel at seminary, it was a start, but I still flung — still fling — myself from morning prayers straight into frenetic activity. I'm practicing, with firm intention, bringing the slowness of the liturgy into the rest of my day. This is how time expands. This is how we become living poetry.

The elevation of the Host almost literally stops time. At such moments, the entire cosmos steps to the precipice. Will we fly yet again? I could cram centuries into the interval when, celebrating the Mass, I lift the Host. I hardly quite know when I place it on the paten again. Love, it seems, has a gravity all its own. I may as well crawl home.

✠ ✠ ✠

Poetry is slow. More powerful than prose, poetry stares directly at the sun until you blink. Poetic life is pure combustion, so be careful how you live. You are more than the sum of your parts.

The Mass is slowest of all. Here, we are remade in God's greatest creative act. Blood poured from His side, the New Adam crucified and risen shakes us to ruin and rebuilds us just as our Lord rebuilt His temple in three days. The Mass is the ordinary means by which the incarnate image of Christ is placed upon us to bring us to participate in reality itself, the fullness of reality lived in the freedom and knowledge of Christ. This is possible in Christ alone.

The Blessed Sacrament isn't a mere symbol or feel-good Sunday morning moment. It's the gate through which the human soul is joined to God. His image remakes us and we're invited, through grace, into the trinitarian sharing of perfect familial love. When you step up to the communion rail to receive, be sure you're confessed, moderate your pace, and watch your step.

The transcendent God breaking into time is radically creative. The old is torn out by the roots. We aren't dragged out of time by His transcendence. Rather, Christ brings all of time with Him and joins us to it. He arrives with living memory, memory not content to remain in the past.

The Cross stands before our eyes even as the Resurrected Lord shines. Calvary isn't a long-past historical event. We participate in the sacrifice directly, poetically. What I mean by this is that poetics is an examination of making, and our Lord's sacrifice remakes time itself, redeeming every moment of history and leading us into eternal glory. The Cross is always present on the altar, always making us, forever a terrible and mighty poem to be read in greater depth.

The poetics of the Cross calls forth, through the power of sacrament, the living image of Christ. By *image*, I don't simply mean a picture, an idea we hold in our minds. I mean a spark, a solar flash of supernatural intuition, a sideways glance at the font of Being. An image is a form of knowledge that's very real but for which we have no logical explanation. When we talk about the image of Christ, it doesn't remain only in the imagination. Because of who He is, it can't. He's prior to the imagination, before metaphor, before language. Remember, before the Word ever speaks the world into existence, He *is*.

His image is inexhaustible. A good metaphor in a poem seems inexhaustible, but, really, it's more like an open door, an occasion for discovery. Metaphor is how we put two parts together and attempt to express an idea by creating a third thing, a new concept buried in the relation of the parts — my love is a rose, your eyes are pearls, and so on. The reality underlying the sacraments is this but so much more. It's an unbounded and dangerous reality. To look directly at the face of God is deadly. We can't handle that direct experience yet, so He gives us the sacraments.

The image of Christ doesn't have parts. It's a transparent, true reflection of inexhaustible grace. The Eucharist doesn't have parts. It's pure. We are meant to gaze at Christ and accept His Body and Blood, not to tug at Him to see how He's held together. Metaphor you can snip at in certain ways. You can't snip at an image. We have Christ or we have nothing.

Here's what really stops me dead in my tracks. Christ, by His very nature, takes on flesh. The way Aquinas explains it is that God the Father eternally forms this image in His mind and the image is so perfect, so full of love, that it cannot help but to be the Son. It cannot remain theoretical.

The image of Christ demands incarnation. His Body and Blood are *real*. We hold the Blessed Sacrament on our tongue, sweet as honey. It feeds us. As the language of transformation, it gets inside us and rewrites us. The image is taken on personally as we become new creations, each one an image of Christ, walking poems communicating God's love wherever we go.

I find the responsibility unnerving. It forms a strong contrast with the boredom of sin and exhaustion of godlessness. Maybe that's why

Plato tosses the poets outside the city gates, the Roman emperors rounded up Christians and fed them to lions, and Queen Elizabeth petulantly tried to stamp the Mass out. It's dangerous stuff. As Baldwin of Canterbury says, "When this word is spoken, its message pierces the heart like the sharp arrows of a strong man, like nails driven deep."

☩ ☩ ☩

The poetry of Gerard Manley Hopkins, in particular, startles me. Partly it's his skill as a writer, of course — the way he uses rhythm and alliteration to slow down readers. I read the same line repeatedly before catching his meaning.

He also makes up his own words, smashing them together and reconstructing the pieces. All the great poets do it. Shakespeare, for instance, invented countless words and phrases. He was the first to fight fire with fire and warn about the green-eyed monster. Hopkins is more partial to hitching words together with a dash. He writes about clouds that "Chevy on an air-built thoroughfare," and how the "million-fueled, / nature's bonfire burns on."

He doesn't create words because he doesn't know how to use a dictionary. Having searched far and wide, he discovers the right word doesn't yet exist. He's an explorer. His poems exert gravity. They pull me into orbit. I stare at them, wish I had written them, then shake my head in wonder. The poems aren't mine, so possessive thoughts are out of place. Better to explore what the poem changes in me and why I love it so.

Not long ago, I read a Hopkins poem about the leaves falling off the trees in autumn. All the best poems are about common themes. This one is for a young girl:

Margaret, are you grieving
Over Goldengrove unleaving?

Already, an invented word — unleaving — the action of a leaf falling from a branch. Unleaving invokes departure. When combined with the *go* sound twice repeated in Goldengrove, it creates nostalgia. A golden grove is forever left behind, lost behind a closed door. Eden must be abandoned, and even children grow old. Hopkins mourns lost beauty, heartsick that we unleave from this world.

Hopkins is concerned that, as we age and become cynical, we're immunized to the sadness of departure:

> Though worlds of wanwood leafmeal lie;
> And yet you will weep and know why.
> Now no matter, child, the name:
> Sorrow's springs are the same.

He grieves more than the pilgrimage of a leaf from branch to soil. He's writing about the ghost of lost innocence and the inevitable drift of our bodies toward death;

> Nor mouth had, no nor mind, expressed
> What heart heard of, ghost guessed:
> It is the blight man was born for,
> It is Margaret you mourn for.

It's a simple poem, but I return to it again and again. When depressed about lost friends, wasted time, the advance of gray hairs on my head, the new pain in my knee, the thought of my children growing old and moving away from home, this is the kind of poem that assures I'm not alone even as I flutter like a leaf, torn and faded.

Here's another simple line of poetry — "Hoc est enim corpus meum" — I recite it every day. I never tire of it. The Roman Missal instructs the priest to say the words slowly, clearly, and deliberately. It simply won't do to hurry. I suppose I could make an intellectual attempt to explain why they affect me so. But I can't. I really can't.

There's always something new in them. All I can do is repeat them yet again.

When I celebrate the Mass, the words aren't an exterior reality to which I adapt—that's only the beginning stage of interpreting the poem. They embrace me as reality in which to participate. This is true knowledge. The words don't tell me *about* our Lord; they wrap me in His love.

"Hoc est enim corpus meum" are words of unleaving, birth and death, calling us into being like Christ calling into the void. Occasionally, the words catch in my throat. I hesitate. I've even cried.

We are leaves falling from the tree.

✠ ✠ ✠

Coleridge says that poetry is the best words in the best order. Each word affects the next. A word on its own is a wondrous thing, but two words next to each other generate so much friction they catch fire.

This marks me as a stubborn curmudgeon to admit, but when I celebrate the Mass I vastly prefer the Roman Canon, which is the first Eucharistic Prayer. The Canon has been handed down by our ancestors and has nurtured countless saints. Praying it is a continuing sign of unity with them. We don't need new, diversionary prayers. Different options every day at the Mass for the sake of variety is unnecessary. My only desire is to respect and guard the beauty of the perfect poem handed down by the saints. The best words in the best order.

In repetition it gains power, but never becomes rote. I regularly tell my wife that I love her. Every day, the same three words, a repetition representing increased faithfulness. I'm still here. I still love you. Similarly, I regularly tell God I love Him. I say it the same way, with the Mass, carving out a decades-long pattern I never intend to cease.

Now, the Roman Canon is longer than the other Eucharistic Prayers, by about two minutes. People have literally brought stopwatches to Masses—not mine—and checked. Occasionally, before they learned not to—because I'll talk forever once on a soapbox—people would ask why I don't use the shorter prayers. I tell them my sense is that we have the extra two minutes. In any case, I'd rather cut the homily. My words aren't so important, but the Roman Canon is pure poetry.

There is, of course, the repetition of the *Hoc est* no matter which Eucharistic Prayer is employed. The slower Roman Canon, though, provides opportunity to latch onto the repetition and appreciate it. There are other repetitions as well. Listen carefully. How many times do you hear the words *sacrifice, peace, gift*? Where do the words appear? What words are next to them? How do the words change? How have they changed since you heard them last week?

Repetition isn't retreat to familiarity. Rather, it reveals the next step forward. A poem becomes increasingly meaningful. The Mass ripens new fruit each time we return. We ourselves don't arrive the same as we were yesterday. Even more true, we never leave a Mass the same as we entered it. In a modest hour of time we travel an unimaginable distance.

The vast interior distance traveled is possible only by pausing with the poem. Novelty and haste keep us frozen. As we rush around doing errands, scrolling social media, overworking, commuting, gossiping, wishing Mass would be shorter, it might be wise to wonder why we're in such a hurry. Where, exactly, are we going? Why so anxious to move?

I've always struggled with the need to be productive. Because of this, I hate going slow when I could be going fast. I have a relentless need to move before I'm ready and can only conclude that I'm addicted to newness. In the past, I itched to abandon myself because I didn't like myself. Maybe something new would be better. If nothing else, the illusion of progress would alleviate true self-examination.

The inability to slow down infects our worship. It's apparent in our appetite for ever-new music oriented toward entertainment, parish-hopping to avoid commitment to a specific community, and regularly changing the words of the Mass to enhance novelty. By not staying still, we can claim we're hard at work on evangelization and church growth or whatever other buzz words are ascendant, but none of the progress is real. The Church will continue to hemorrhage parishioners until we slow down and attend to the Mass. God is asking us to watch and wait with Him.

I'm not championing blind nostalgia. Repetition isn't in thrall to a golden age that never existed. The Mass isn't a museum, and our repeated, careful, and reverent remembrance of Christ isn't sentiment or dead tradition.

When I receive the Eucharist, I'm brought to a restful place in which I'm authentically myself, left without defense before the Lord. He knows me and yet continues to love me. There's no hurry to leave this grace-filled spiritual state. In fact, no one ever claimed it must be left at all. After all, contemplation and action spring from the same source.

The philosopher Søren Kierkegaard, in his book *Repetition*, recommends listening closely to those differences in ourselves that are revealed through repetition. We discover in the differences an entirely new manner of thinking.

My old manner of thinking was impatient of the idea of repetition. I couldn't slow down because it felt wrong. It felt that way because I couldn't appreciate the differences in myself. I was eager for instant progress and cheap grace, wanting to exchange one experience for another. I was willing to throw out everything that made me who I was in order to possess new experiences like tourist trinkets. I wanted to possess each experience, all on my own, and be free to trade it in for new ones if I so desired. There was no value, in my mind, to covering the same ground again, but repetition, poetically experienced, unravels the hasty need to possess. Two experiences overlap each other without asking anything of the other. Two Masses can be exactly the same and yet each has individual value, each has something to give.

As I've uncovered the value of repetition, I've accepted the responsibility to give, not take. To each Mass, to God, to my brothers and sisters who pray with me, to the entire world, I give my love. I ask nothing more. I don't need to rush. I don't need to receive anything. I don't need to be entertained by novelty. The Holy Sacrifice is the poem I will read until the day I die, because it is the limitless unfolding of possibility.

In the story of our lives, the Mass puts our best words in the best order. One after another. Thus are we brought, piece by piece, bone to flesh, to the side of Christ.

☩ ☩ ☩

As a freshly graduated student with chrism still fragrant on my palms, I thought of pastoring a church in abstract terms. I hadn't yet held the hand of a dying parishioner and then cried in the hospital elevator, proposed an annual budget backed by only three months of funds, negotiated an insolvable disagreement between spouses, or had to apologize for being a bad pastor. I had a head stuffed with theology but hadn't endured the brackish Cape wind that rattles through the cedar shingles in false spring or stepped on the broken salt-crusted oyster shells of my new parish.

Language these days is awfully abstract. We speak and think in sweeping euphemisms, self-censoring and masking our true thoughts. Even worse, perhaps we're incapable of saying what we really think because we're not thinking all that much. The more abstract language is, the less poetic. It may be more functional, so abstraction has its place, but it's less useful in a real sense. It lacks concreteness. It lacks love.

When we love someone or something, we want to know everything, every detail. I can tell you that my wife's fondest wish is to have a personal chef, that she stays up late at night embroidering vestments, and that it doesn't take much to make her happy. I can tell you a thousand other details, and I want to know more. The specific, quirky details are what make her Amber, my wife. She isn't an abstract idea of a woman.

If you come to Epiphany and assist at the Mass, I hope you would be able to observe that, in my heart, I'm trying my best to love God because it outwardly shows in my specific actions. You could observe me carefully unfold the corporal, hold my fingers pressed together after touching the Blessed Sacrament, and then scrape the corporal with the paten. You may overhear my quietly whispered secret prayers. You would surely notice the exquisite vestments and appreciate the absence of chit-chat. I'm slow, deliberately unhurried. This way, I won't neglect any detail, because no detail is insignificant. It's a love language, the way a priest offers a Mass.

When you're in love, abstraction simply won't do. God doesn't love humanity. He loves me. He loves you. He counts the hairs on your head, even the gray ones, keeping each one safe.

When I arrived on Cape Cod, I fell in love with my parish. Over time, each parishioner sharpened in relief and became unique. We shared specific experiences, had our ups and downs—they made me frustrated and they made me happy. We prayed together about concerns they brought to me; we went bass fishing over the sandbars off Monomoy. I baptized their babies. Some I buried.

The only language concrete enough to bear the weight of love is poetic. Poetry carries the significance of a relationship between two friends, man and wife, Heavenly Father and child. Nothing else will do. We sing, says St. Augustine, because songs are for lovers.

When I was thrown into active ministry, I couldn't love my parish in the abstract. My spiritual fatherhood demanded I know them intimately. This was a lesson I was happy to learn. What wasn't so easy, though, was applying that same insight to my relationship with God. For years, I'd been distancing myself from Him. I know that sounds odd. After all, I'm telling you the story of how I became a pastor of a church, but my love for God had become shallow. It was abstract.

I liked the idea of God. I even trusted that idea, but past experiences of hurt had made me cautious about becoming personally engaged. Pastors had disappointed and offended me. I transferred my anger toward them onto God. I knew He wasn't to blame but couldn't help but feel that the personal, invite-Jesus-into-your-heart brand of religion associated with my past was somehow mixed up with it all. Easier to abandon that past and quickly move on. I still fervently believed in God and even loved Him, but I didn't want it to be personal. That's not how love works, though. Love has to be personal. This is why our Lord took on flesh. Love demands it.

Sin is opposite. Sin is not only harmful, it's harmfully boring. It erases everything that makes us special and abstracts us into material objects, statistics, consumers, advertising demographics. Sin makes us manipulable, subject to joining faceless crowds.

I thought I was going to minister to my new parish. In their own way, though, each one of my parishioners ministered to me as well. For that I'm grateful. They gave me love. In that love, delivered uniquely as only each individual could love—an invitation for a cup of coffee, an encouraging word, a ride to the airport—there was a revelation of the common love that binds the communion of saints into a single body. "Christ plays in ten thousand places," writes Hopkins, "Lovely in limbs, and lovely in eyes not his / To the Father through the features of men's faces."

My parishioners thought they were simply providing small acts of kindness, but what they did was much more. They assisted God to love me. Through them, God made clear that He really does love me and my relationship with Him can be personal. It was poetry in action.

✠ ✠ ✠

At our rural family property, I take walks with my daughter. She's barely more than a toddler and progresses slowly even when her little legs are working hard. Often, I carry her along for a bit until she wriggles from my arms again. These walks are for the purpose of discovering "interesting things" in the woods and along the streams that cut into the sandstone hills like veins. In spring, the water from Midwestern thunderstorms pours down the hills in sheets and the streams rise and spread onto shallow tables of rock or onto fields of new-planted seed. Over hundreds of years, the topsoil has been carried down into the valleys, exposing the bones of the hillsides. The oak trees and grape vines stubbornly mine the thin soil for nutrients and slowly crack the bedrock with their roots.

My daughter stops and points to an old tire just off the path in the woods, basically a piece of garbage the previous owners left behind. "A black snake lived there last summer," she tells me. "He was inside of it." I nod my head in assent. I hadn't known this. We move on. A few more steps down the path and she lets go of my hand again. She's crouching down, pointing. It's a mushroom tucked into the roots of an oak. She knows this place.

We take walks back home in our urban neighborhood, too. We circle the block. She points out houses to me, saying, "That's a cat window," and, "That's 'nother cat window." These are windows where cats can often be found sitting on the sill. I hadn't known this, but she even knows by the specific cat windows when we're getting close to the gated steps leading into our yard. By slowing down, she has intimately inhabited the neighborhood. She knows when home is near.

This is why I take precise care of every single detail of the Mass. Some people are patiently watching for the snake tires and cat windows.

✠ ✠ ✠

Memory is the stuff of who we are. We all tell stories about where we came from. These stories shape our identity. Memories can and do change over time. Some fall away. Some gain sharpness and definition. They shift our conception of the present moment, how we interact with others, what our goals are, what possibilities the future holds.

Memory ripens like plucked blueberries, tasting of both sun and dirt. Shakespeare writes about the feeling:

When to the sessions of sweet silent thought
I summon up remembrance of things past,
I sigh the lack of many a thing I sought,
And with old woes new wail my dear time's waste.

Memory relives the past even as it slips away, a precious but fragile treasure to be guarded and protected. There are certain memories I hold dear, experiences that, even as they unfold, make me mutter, "Remember this. Remember this."

I remember the feeling of my grandfather's hand, shaped by years of cotton farming in southern Missouri, the last time I held it. I relive laughing with family around the fire on a summer night, roasting marshmallows with sticky hands and faces. I picture our toddlers striding with the carriage of cavemen while their mother and I praise their gracefulness. I'll never forget the clouds wreathing the Blue Ridge Mountains and the earth cradling the sky below Clingman's Dome the morning I bicycled through town and up the side of a mountain. We all have peaks that stand out from the mist. Eventually, we descend back into the valley. This is the bittersweetness of memory.

Every garden has a serpent, every Easter a Lent. If you would gain your soul, our Lord is clear: you must first lose everything. To attain eternal life, we must leave the old at the foot of the Cross. If we would travel to Heaven, we must mark a path behind. As we travel, it's all about what we remember.

The exile metaphor unravels like a scarlet thread through the Mass. We slide into the shelter of God's wing, but cannot remain there. Soon enough, we're thrust out of the nest. Even the scarlet thread perishes, for God has commanded it tossed onto the sacrificial bonfire. It's exile upon exile. Some memories must perish. Perhaps this is why God is so insistent that He forgets all our sins.

Adam and Eve leave home wrapped in animal skins as their only protection, carrying humanity with them. Our journey starts outside of Eden, marked by the weight of that first sin. All our lives, we sneak peeks over the shoulder, desperate to turn and run home. So many of my parishioners think something is wrong with them because they're unsettled, lonely, and alienated. In fact, we all share those experiences, every single one of us, and what's wrong is sin. It poisons our memory and drags us backward. We have to hold our memories lightly, cherishing them for what they are but always picking them up and carrying them forward.

The Church draws a connection between exile from Eden and the temptation of our Lord. Christ in the desert is a replay of the wandering and homeless Israelites. The Church strides the same path, but with the assurance that our Lord enters the desert with us. If you're like me, you're probably walking Him in circles.

It would be a betrayal for me, as a priest, to pretend the Christian life is painless. The Scriptures make clear that we're wounded by sin. We can delude ourselves, I suppose. We're good at that. But the lies are exactly what propelled us from Eden, the refusal to take a good honest look at who we are and who we are not.

The repetitive nature of sin is only countered by a corresponding repetition of virtue. Slow down — return to the Mass again and again. Go to Confession and don't be discouraged about bringing the same list of sins as last time. Walk those circles with Christ.

The memory of sin is a heavy burden, so we salve our conscience by pretending our sins aren't all that bad; everybody else is doing it so it must be okay — I know I excuse myself in those exact ways — but these are the lies that continue to keep us far from home. Don't forget your sins until God takes them away. Face them. Remember them. Allow God to forgive them. Then, once He does, toss them to the western wind.

In, "The Peace of Wild Things," Wendell Berry writes,

When despair grows in me
and I wake in the night at the least sound
in fear of what my life and my children's lives may be,
I go and lie down where the wood drake rests.

There, sitting by still water, he reconnects with God. Supernatural peace drives away anxiety, temptation, distraction, feelings of inadequacy, and fear of the future. The Mass is still water. When you're unsettled, pause there with God and remember.

Remember this, Christ is the only Bread we need. His sustenance is portioned out in every good thing, every beautiful memory.

Remember this. We still sin but will be forgiven if we only think to ask. We are not in Eden. Better, we're on the path home. We're not perfect but we are loved. Remember.

✠ ✠ ✠

After five happy years on Cape Cod, our lives took a drastic swerve. This was our conversion to Catholicism, selling our first home, moving to St. Louis, and saying goodbye to the life we'd built.

All those experiences of visiting the Mass had finally gotten under my skin, so deeply that I felt almost compelled to convert. There is no easy explanation why it happened. Although I feel it was a rational decision, there was no particular intellectual reason, no Catholic doctrine I finally resolved. Simply put, I was converted by beauty. It was very similar to falling in love.

At the time, I wrote an essay for the website *Called to Communion*. In it, I said that I might be able to offer a decent defense of the various theological reasons why I came into the Catholic Church, but my preference — then and now — is to say simply that the visible, undivided Church, the Church that Jesus prays for in His last moments with His disciples, the Church that is the Mother of us all because she holds Christ within her womb; this I recognize by the way that she walks. The truth of her beliefs is radiant and alive.

This isn't to say that being received into the Catholic Church was easy. For me, the physical expression of the inner turmoil I felt will always be the St. Vincent de Paul chapel.

The chapel was designed for seminarians but is now mainly used by employees of the St. Louis curia. The seminarians are down the street in a new building, but signs of the building's former purpose are etched into the architecture. One wing is marked with a carved stone plaque for philosophers, and the other is set aside for theologians. The division refers to the separation of the major and minor seminaries. Philosophy is always before theology. As the lower science, it's learned first and becomes foundational.

Along the perimeter of the chapel, the aisles are lined with at least a dozen side altars. This is where the seminarians practiced and, I imagine, the seminary priests offered concurrent Masses back in the days before the rubrics allowed concelebration. Filling most of the interior space, bounded by a carved wood enclosure, is the choir, lined with three ascending rows of seats. The seats face across the center aisle, situated for a schola of seminarians to chant the Propers of the Mass and the Psalms of the Daily Office back and forth to each other.

When I began working for the archdiocese, I'd left Anglicanism behind and could no longer call myself a pastor. I use the word *pastor*, but I'd very much considered myself a priest. One of my fiercest interior struggles in joining the Church was leaving my priestly identity behind. There was a real chance I would no longer wear a collar, serve at the altar, or hear a confession again. My priesthood meant everything to me. It's how I defined myself. I was a priest.

Having discerned the truth of the Church's claims by her beauty, I came to think of her as my Mother. What child would keep distance from his Mother? I needed to enter the Church. So, for the sake of my salvation and that of our young children, I relinquished the priesthood. Our family was received into the Church and we've never regretted it for an instant.

Soon enough, though, it became clear I labored under a misconception. I thought I owned the identity of *priest*. I consider it somehow mine, hard-won through years of study and service. I wept to leave priesthood behind. I didn't understand why I had to; even as I entered the Church I resented her ways. But we must be willing to abandon everything for God, and so I came to Him with empty hands, humiliated.

I was a layman.

I worked in the archdiocesan offices and attended Mass in the chapel of St. Vincent de Paul every day. Because the seats were built as a choir, we perched on the seats at an angle and craned our necks to view the altar. After a while, I simply knelt straight ahead and closed my eyes. I didn't need to see a picture of what I'd lost.

Over the course of four months, a rotation of priests offered Masses. I, of course, was not one of them. I sat, frustrated, in tweed jacket and club tie. No cassock. No white collar. Those weren't for me anymore. Clothes reveal a lot about the person wearing them, and mine said, firmly and unequivocally, that I was not a priest.

That's not even the worst part. During those first months in St. Louis, I wasn't formally a Catholic yet. For four months, day after day, I attended Mass and wasn't able to receive the Eucharist. The Catholics around me filed out of the choir stalls, stepped past while I twisted my knees out of the way, approached the altar, and received the Sacrament.

Amber and I had a mentor over the course of those months. Amber has always been sanguine, so she took it all in stride. I'm melancholic. I felt the hurt of being denied the Sacrament. In our meetings I ranted and raved. I pleaded. I whined. Our mentor was unmoved by my protestations and refused to move the date of our reception into the Church forward. He explained that being forced to slow down was good for me. I needed to feel the cost of schism and was being given the opportunity to participate in the wounds inflicted upon the Body of Christ.

He was right. Sometimes, when we slow down, God reveals difficult truths. As Edith Stein says, "When we are reduced to nothingness in the highest degree of humility, then the spiritual union of the soul with God takes place."

☩ ☩ ☩

Hopkins grieves Goldengrove as the loss of home. As much as we love family, friends, houses, and parishes, we cannot stay forever.

We age. Life moves on. Children grow up and move away. Our physical health declines. We go to the grave.

I noticed this at our most recent family Thanksgiving. So much has changed; an entire older generation has departed and been replaced. We recently sold my grandparents' home after my grandfather died. I'll never be there for Thanksgiving again, never warm my back at the fireplace at Christmas as my grandfather throws wrapping paper into the fire. In some way, I'll always be that young child by the fireplace.

Beauty rips at my heart and, when I look back, it's with joyful sadness. I cannot go to college for the first time again or relive becoming a father for the first time. I cried when we left Cape Cod. Three of my children were born there. We ate pizza on the beach. I built a new room with my dad. I became an adult there in that house. For me, it's Goldengrove. I solemnly vowed after that experience to never move again.

In spite of my best efforts, I've said goodbye to several parishes through the normal course of priest transfers. I hate it, it never gets easier, but we cannot be home to all the people and places to whom we want to be home. Our fundamental human condition is to be travelers.

Ever since sin thrust us from Eden, we've been walking. All is not lost, though. Beauty reconnects us to those experiences. But here, as with everything else, we cannot stay. Pope Benedict calls this the pain of nostalgia. *Nostalgia* literally means to be *homesick*. Beauty points us home but cannot permanently provide shelter. It drives an arrow into the heart. Beauty hurts.

The Mass hurts. It causes homesickness. Maybe that's why we speed through it carelessly, to avoid the sting of entering heavenly reality and then returning to ordinary life. It's easier never to feel than to suffer unrequited longing. Those feelings, though, shouldn't cause us to draw back. Rather, seek more. The suffering of beauty wakes us up to our true home. In the New Jerusalem we will be held in the strong arms of Christ, together, where we belong.

If I rush through the Mass, I don't suffer the dull ache of beauty which reassures me that somewhere, at the end of the journey, there's a place for me. Slowing down is but the first effort in learning to stop entirely. Stop my whirling, colliding, anxious thoughts. Stop with the doubt and distraction. Stop. Rest. For now, we have a long way to go, but it won't always be this way.

✠ ✠ ✠

The drawn-out wait to participate more fully in the Mass made me anxious. I learned to accept it, but constantly struggled. God never makes us wait for the sake of waiting, though, and even if we cannot comprehend the purpose, there always is one. God doesn't place ambiguity on us. He prefers clarity over confusion, but He will use it for good if we cooperate. Sin races ahead, takes what it wants, and by doing so entirely halts spiritual progress. That's why so many people feel stuck. On the other hand, voluntarily slowing down to wait with God is the secret to spiritual progress. Before we go, we must stop.

The Mass isn't slow for the sake of slowness. It isn't out-of-touch, fussy, or irrelevant to our fast-paced society. Liturgy is slow because it moves Heaven and earth. It's traveling an infinite distance.

Paul Claudel, in *A Poet Before the Cross*, writes that God is passing through our midst. To catch sight of Him we must endure "the Waiting of all the centuries." During the three years Christ ministered in Israel, the anticipation of centuries is constricted and pushed into exasperation. Everyone has been waiting for the Messiah, and now they clamor for miracles, an armed revolt, seizure of power, something, anything. All Israel joined the Psalmist: "O my God, make haste to help me!" (Ps. 71:12).

Christ knows His business. He disappears into the desert for forty days, wanders alone on mountaintops, paces the surface of the sea. The people wait. For three years. Finally, our Lord turns His face to Jerusalem where, in response to waving palms and cries of hosanna, He lays down His life and dies. Oddly enough, it all happens too quickly.

As I waited in the St. Vincent de Paul chapel—not a priest, not receiving the Eucharist—Christ was present, but not in the way I wanted. He invited me to sit with Him for a while in a midnight garden. He offered to share a cross. The waiting was the opportunity of a century.

Lingering patiently with Christ is the height of dramatic movement. All poetry is movement, but the Mass moves us faster and further than we could ever dream. There's tension in the glacial buildup as we prepare to leave time behind. The priest pauses at the foot of the altar, hesitant, and makes a *Confiteor*. There's no rush to step up and kiss it. Those opening words, the invitation into the heart of the Trinity via the Passion of our Lord. The drama of the Scriptures sung to the lightless north. The slow burn of the Roman Canon. The incense drifting. The chant like a mother's lullaby. It's strictly controlled, chaste beauty, and for all that it gains intensity until it flares when the priest holds the Host aloft. The universe turns on its axis around the Victim. A tidal wave of silence, like the afternoon of our Lord's Crucifixion, erupts like an abyss, a slight intake of breath, our held breath as we burn under the intensity of His gaze.

This is our Lord, the one for whom we have waited centuries. He is in our midst. "The moment has come to speak clearly," says Claudel. Christ enters His temple, bearing down with divine weight. Claudel becomes prophetic, "Speak, speak, Israel! You are needed. There is no backing down now. It is up to you to utter the sacramental Yes."

✠ ✠ ✠

A Mass cannot be explained like a fact. It's meant to be lived. There's no shortcut. All we can do is allow the poem to carry us as Christ, the Poet, creates. His making, still in progress, is you and me.

What is He unconcealing? What possibility for us all of creation is founded upon God's divine truth?

The Word holds secrets behind His back.

To read this sacred poetry and locate my origin in it, I take a hard look inside my soul. Each word, each symbolic action, is laden with deep meaning in regard to human destiny. In the Sacrament, we not only have an admirable example of poetic mystery, but we have *the* foundational mystery, Christ's abiding, beautiful sacramental presence.

The Sacrament extends grace from Poet to reader. We are brought into the beauty of the Mass even when we aren't prepared — we're never prepared — such is our Lord's kindness. He only asks that we arrive. Slow down enough to be there. He will be for us poet and priest, sacrifice and mystery.

The Mass bestows meaning on every aspect of our existence. It is the meaning-maker.

The Mass is still water. Rest. Remember.

The Word of His heart, returning to His heart.

FIVE
The Sun in My Hands

SUNRISE SPILLS THROUGH the alleys between the houses across the street from mine. Our house is a nineteenth-century Victorian beauty adorned with patterned terra-cotta and antique stained glass. Her bones are red brick, fired from clay dug out of nearby hills by Sicilian immigrants. The houses in our neighborhood are older than the street grid and charmingly align at an angle that's a few degrees off. Our whole neighborhood, Benton Park, is perched on top of subterranean lager-brewing caves that honeycomb the bluff overlooking the western shore of the Mississippi. Each morning, the sun separates from the river over the neon sign of the brewery. The beams find me already ensconced in my faded damask wingback chair by the fireplace, reading a book with a cup of coffee in hand. These days, I'm quite happy to wake in the dark.

It wasn't always this way. As a younger man, I stayed up late hours oil painting to sad songs on the record player. A melancholic night owl, the perfect caricature of a tortured artist, to me poetry was all emotion, sadness, and overwrought passion. This belief was a reflection of my state of mind. Thoughts piled and jumbled and wrestled in my brain and I had nowhere to put them.

In those months of waiting in the St. Vincent de Paul chapel before reception into the Church, I'd already intellectually assented to her teachings. Even though beauty was the main appeal, her truth was quite lovely as well. The medievals, in fact, refer to beauty as the splendor of truth.

I'd recognized that truth. In response to it, our little family relocated halfway across the United States in order to become Catholic and explore the possibility that I might become a Catholic priest in the Archdiocese of St. Louis. I had peace about this.

At the same time, as I've indicated, a shadow lingered over me. On Sundays, we attended Mass at the local parish as a family. I watched as if I were the audience for a play. I had some inkling that I wasn't there for entertainment and the sanctuary isn't a stage. I'd already formed my thoughts in that direction. I was aware our position as outsiders wouldn't last forever, but my intellectual assent was still superficial. I didn't yet *know* the Church. I hadn't yet seen how expansive she is from the inside. I'd intuited Christ's beauty but hadn't sat down at His banqueting table.

It was, I would guess, five or so years of growing in recognition that the Mass is poetic. In fact, my whole existence is poetic. Christ, as poet, is hotly pursuing us. We are not mere facts to Him, but beloved creations. We are a result of divine act. As we search for Him, He calls out, searching longer and more persistently.

It's been fascinating for me to look back and discern the shape of that journey. I have my story and I know you have yours. The only thing required is that you become convinced of how important your story truly is, and that you can live a truly, stunningly beautiful life.

In Christ, we wake earlier and earlier, trim the wicks of our lamps, and are content to wait later and later into the night. At this point, I'm happy to wait forever, if need be. The Bridegroom, I know, is just outside the door. He rises like the sun.

✠ ✠ ✠

All things that exist, to the extent they exist, are good. All material creatures, including human beings, participate in God's goodness through the goodness of existence He bestows. The fact that we *are* instead of *are not* has symbolic heft. It points the way back to God, the One Who Exists. The great I Am.

What does it mean to be written into existence by the divine hand? And to know that our existence somehow, through the Mass, mysteriously connects to the very existence of Almighty God?

My goodness, friends.

Insomniac that I am, I sometimes lie awake at night fretting over the end of physical existence. The thought of death is too much. My heart shivers, the bony winter branches of the crabapple scrape the window, and I can't fall asleep.

Fear of the unknown causes doubt. I lose the connection, the thread that binds me to God, but it seems tragically unfaithful to prod my finger into His wounded side and injure His precious heart. So guilt piles on top of melancholy.

Many seem to have the opposite problem. They hardly give eternal life a thought, living in a constant state of death-denial, lazily assuming they'll last forever. Gertrud von Le Fort, in *The Eternal Woman*, says, "Only an age profoundly bewildered or misled in its metaphysical instincts could attribute the idea of eternity ... to a creature." Misunderstanding our relation to eternity annihilates our humanity. It makes us into, as Wallace Stevens might say, emperors of ice cream.

There's no denying that we are creatures born to die. Our souls are fitted to Heaven and push against our present condition like butterfly wings against a chrysalis. We're designed to embrace the consuming flame of love that gives meaning to death. Here, in a supremely ironic twist, is the link between this life and the next. A voluntary death before our inevitable, actual death.

If metaphysical significance is grasped only through relation to the divine, then the world is analogical. What I mean by this is simple—everything, absolutely everything, finds its meaning in God. If any of our days here on earth are beautiful or good, true, full of happiness and meaning, it's only because we're reflecting, through analogical participation, the God who is Beauty. His transcendence breaks through in our humble, small acts of finite beauty. An abstract idea of beauty won't do. God works purely, poetically, in our specific and unique gifts.

This thought is awe-inspiring but doesn't necessarily help me fall asleep at night. It does, however, bring contentment at the necessity of both sunrises and sunsets.

"It is only great art in its supreme moments of inspiration that is capable of proclaiming under a transitory form the things that are unchanging," Le Fort writes. Beauty is encounter with eternity.

The encounter is sourced and shaped by the sacramental nature of the Mass.

As revelation of supreme beauty, the Mass bridges eternity and time, simultaneously humbles and exalts, lowering hills to valleys and valleys to hills, setting us on the horizon of eternity as it veils and unveils. I don't find this situation easy. I would like to know that my intellectual assent to the Faith is enough and to be secure in my conception of God as an idea. I desire consistent, measurable spiritual progress.

Instead, God offers Himself. Beauty. The sacraments. A ladder descending from Heaven, thronged with angels.

✠ ✠ ✠

A few months ago, I had a custom red and gold silk fabric milled for new vestments. I agonized over the details—the cut and shape, the gold embroidery on the humeral veil. The vestments, once completed, were stunning. They were also costly. Wearing them makes me feel like the Magdalene pouring away her best perfume.

Liturgically, I strive to use the best incense, hold the candles in gleaming candlesticks, and spare no expense for cut flowers. The flowers are slain as a sacrifice to our Lord. The incense is crushed and burned away. The time I spend in those vestments cannot be recovered. I use the minutes and they're gone. It's gratuitous, this precious, dying beauty we offer to God. Many see tragedy in the waste. I see poetry, pure gift.

The greater the sacrifice, the greater the love. Love, like beauty, is gratuitous. It seems unnecessary to the business of life, but, really, it's all we live for.

Aristotle describes human creativity as imitation, our making as an artifice that mimics nature. St. John Henry Newman doesn't contradict him, but clarifies that poetics is more than an explanation of reproduction. The beauty we make is a representation of the ideal. It stretches out to contact an entirely other world.

Beauty doesn't follow a pattern. It's a language deeper than fact, more descriptive than history. "The poetical mind," says Newman, "is one full of the eternal forms of beauty and perfection." Beauty elevates earth to Heaven, a staggering feat, which is why glassy seas and high mountain vistas overwhelm, why we cry at movies and become strangely euphoric in the presence of live music. An aching love wells up inside us, called forth by beauty from this world and yet not fitting into this world.

The source of it all, the poetic act fullest to overflowing with eternal beauty, is the Mass, which literally accomplishes the miracle of uniting mankind with God. It places eternity and time into the same space and waits for the explosion.

When we receive grace, Christ impresses His form onto us and re-makes us in His image. "Revealed Religion should be especially poetical," says Newman. Then, in a passage of unsurpassed lyricism, he teaches that religion "presents us with those ideal forms of excellence in which a poetical mind delights, and with which all grace and harmony are associated. It brings us into a new world—a world of overpowering interest, of the sublimest views, and the tenderest and purest feelings."

God deserves our absolute best. After all, He's giving His absolute best. The greater the love, the greater the poem. The Mass is the greatest. We cannot live without it.

Paul Claudel, the poet who was converted when he heard plainchant in a French cathedral on Christmas Day, meditates on a priest's chalice, writing that through it, "we open ourselves and Christ descends between the walls of our being." This has always been a mystery, the infinite God who is small enough to fit into our hearts. The Church explains it, as best she can, through the concept of created grace. Grace descends between the walls of our being, reshaping our hearts to receive God's love. It creates a silver thread of grace that we follow, like Jacob or Ariadne, up through infinite armies of angels along the mystical ladder.

This paradox is reflected in the chalice, which Claudel says is "both inexhaustible and measured, a finite container capable of infinite content, the whole which has become our part, according to the astonishing word of Psalm 72:26, God will be eternally my inheritance."

The chalice has height and depth: we can measure the wine poured into it, can see and taste the drink. The inscape of the wine, though, held in the precious silver throne of the chalice, changed as it is into Christ, is an ocean with no floor.

✠ ✠ ✠

When I obsess over mortality or buckle under the weight of my sins, I'm glad to feel the pain of the struggle. If the obstacles to our spiritual progress were insurmountable, and we were all destined as a sinners to our graves, I'd quickly become apathetic. It is hope that makes us suffer.

Hope makes us travelers. It marks us as pilgrims who must be on our way. "It is the inherent 'not yet,'" the philosopher Josef Pieper says, "of the finite being."

The Mass, full of hope, proclaims *not yet*. How beautiful. How frustrating.

The interior dread that keeps me up at night is the orientation toward fulfillment. I know that Catholics have claim to a happy ending, and this destination is precisely how we create the possibility, Pieper says, "of meritorious action, which has the character of genuine 'progress.'" I discover in this the open-endedness of poetry, a constant yearning.

Hell is the opposite, which is why it becomes a very real outcome for the complacent. To cease traveling, to weary of following Christ, is to risk the soul. We must fasten to God alone and never cease struggling to arrive before His face.

"The creatureliness of man reveals itself above all in the deep differentiation of being with regard to God that expresses the fundamental principle of the 'analogy of being,'" says Pieper. What he means is actually quite simple. We are, every single day, called by grace to draw closer to God, and in doing so we draw closer to our own selves.

It's an analogy. We are each, right now, our own selves, but also not quite ourselves. There's no certainty that we will ever fully become ourselves. This goal we only grasp through persistent faith and hope.

At the end of the Mass, the priest sings "Ite, Missa est." Go forth, the Mass is ended. Even as the words are on my lips, I wonder where I'm going and how could it possibly be better than where I am right at that moment.

The fulfillment of hope is tantalizingly near. We want to stay. St. Peter wants to build a hut. It doesn't work that way, though. Hope is Goldengrove.

Robert Frost agrees: "So Eden sank to grief, / So dawn goes down to day. / Nothing gold can stay."

Not yet. Go forth.

☩ ☩ ☩

An analogy bears a whole new meaning, well beyond itself. It's water from Cana.

Analogy is larger on the inside than outside. I wonder if this is why we're so impatient with the Mass. We expect a one-to-one correlation in which we put something in and know exactly what will be offered in return, a trade with measurable value. I give God sacrifice and He responds in a predictable way. The Mass isn't like this. It isn't an exchange of value with God.

When I was in college, I heard a pastor refer to God as a "slot machine." We put in our contribution, pull the lever, and—*bam!*—health, wealth, and success. My past experience with religion burned me out because I'd been taught that God owed specific responses to my expectations. When it didn't happen, I was disillusioned. Religion didn't work for me. Not the way it seemed to be working for other people. It was years before it occurred to me that they we were all playing a game, saying they'd heard from God or leveraging random outcomes to pretend their faith was superior. Everyone was in the same boat and lying to save face.

The Mass, on the other hand, is honest. We lift up our hearts, and all we receive is Christ. That's it. We get all of Him. His suffering and death as well as Resurrection. It's a gift I haven't always wanted, and often it seems like it's disproportionate. I offer God my devotion and in return receive difficulty.

It's a precious gift, though. Disproportionate in all the right ways. It's the chance to suffer with Christ and join our small difficulties to His infinitely valuable sacrifice. I offer my pitiful, small offering and receive eternity in response.

The gate is narrow, but the mansion beyond has uncountable rooms. The gate and the house are somehow related, but only by mystery. We cannot buy entrance.

The Sacrament looks like a piece of bread, but it's shrouded divinity. Over the tabernacle you might notice a covering of colored silk fabric, maybe handmade by some sweet, elderly parishioner. It's actually the boundary between time and eternity, a thing made by a frail and trembling hand. The priest looks a man, but he's the likeness of our Great High Priest. The Mass is but an hour of our time, but it never actually begins or ends.

✠ ✠ ✠

The strange, unabashed imagination of the Church has always attracted me. Growing up, I never "played church" at home the way Catholic children do because our Protestant services were nothing more than a set of hymns followed by an hour of preaching. It was intellectualized, auditory, very adult. My own children play Mass all the time. They think it's fun. Protestant services have very few tangible, imaginative qualities; the Mass, on the other hand, is the font of imagination. This is why the Mass possesses a type of poetic knowledge that cannot be found anywhere else.

One of the children in our parish says that Epiphany "smells like church." The lingering incense triggers a fond memory for him of sacred worship. The parish children wait on pins and needles for the *sanctus* bells. When they sound, the kids give their mothers knowing looks. They knew the whole time the bells would ring. One child recently showed up to worship wearing a cape fashioned from a blanket. She'd seen my *cappa negra* and thought it looked snazzy. The altar boys quarrel over whose turn it is hold the candles in procession. The kids bring flowers to Mary, ponder the stained glass, out-sing the adults on the *Kyrie,* and kneel devoutly at the communion rail. We used to send them out during the homily for kids' church, but now they refuse to leave. We canceled children's church. Our Mass has become so wondrous to the imagination that it is not only reverent and beautiful, it's also kid-friendly. The creativity of Catholicism has captured their attention.

It caught mine, too, in the infancy of my faith journey, long before I converted.

St. Augustine says, "Let our hearts ascend with him," meaning that Christ brings us out of the grave and also to Heaven via the Ascension. When the Host is lifted up during Mass, humanity is lifted up with Him. Christ is our Head. We are the Body. Where He is we are and where He goes we follow. I used to think that, when the bread is consecrated, our Lord comes down into the Host, but that's backwards. The Host draws us upwards, into the furnace of heavenly glory.

God is far different than detractors suppose. He's not angry and isn't out to get us. Even in our sins, He won't reject us. I don't know why God loves us so, but He really does. He takes on human flesh, makes the body sacred, and is born of a mother and father. He has friends. He cries, worries His Mother, and feels the pain of destiny. Maybe as a child He had a dirt bike like I did, built a ramp for it, and bloodied His nose. God is with us in everything we care about—children, family, hobbies, job, the dread that keeps us awake at night, everything.

Through the Mass, God enthrones humanity. People brag about rejecting God. It's the oddest phenomenon—a man sees a priest like me having a cup of coffee at the cafe, minding my own business, and cannot wait to announce that he's dismissed everything I hold dear. The problem is, when these people describe the God they don't believe in, it isn't my God. He's not a distant, demanding patriarch obsessed with obedience and punishment. God is, as Hopkins says, the dayspring to the dimness of us, and a crimson-crested east. Our Lord, in taking on flesh, easters in us, making sacred the human imagination. Paul Claudel, upon inspection and with a little imagination, finds the world to be a symphonic masterpiece:

> Everything is written from margin to margin:
> you could list every little detail, not one syllable lacks.
> The land, the fair sky, the river with its boats,
> cluster of three trees poised over the bank,
> leaf and insect upon the leaf, this stone I toss in my hand,
> village full of people who all speak at once,
> weave and haggle and strike fires, carry their burden,
> complete like an orchestra.

Here's a secret that the godless cannot admit: without God, life is boring. It doesn't sing. Without Christ burning new-born over the horizon, without the Catholic imagination, so suspicious that around every corner hides a love so white-hot it cracks like lightning, a love we only glimpse by the shadow of flame—without this, life is drab.

When my children play Mass, it's because their imaginations are racing. The opposite of a child's play is parody. Children are serious about their games. On the other hand, parodists cannot survive without the source material, which they often mock and attempt to falsify. Of the two, the children are wiser. The Mass is parodied, misrepresented, and appropriated by pop culture because doing so seems edgy and hip. This is actually a capitulation, an acknowledgment that the Church stewards the imagination and, without it, culture is lusterless.

We are able to dream because Christ has returned to Heaven and prepares a place for us. C. S. Lewis says, "I believe in Christianity as I believe the sun has risen, not only because I can see it, but because, by it, I can see everything else." The Mass shifts my focus in such a way that my eyes behold beauty everywhere. On my own, I lacked poetic vision. I didn't see how my present life is already folded into eternity. But now, grounded in the Mass, what I behold—every day, all around—is endlessly fascinating. Claudel exults,

All that is eternity, and the freedom not to be
is all they are deprived of.
I see them with my bodily eyes, produce them in my heart.
My bodily eyes—
In Paradise I should be served by no other eyes!

Chesterton says the imagination makes facts into wonders. The opposite is a mechanized view of the world in which all is functional, abstract, and physical. Our modern era is enslaved by technology, which chases away poetic knowledge. As poetry disappears from daily existence, our days drain out into parody. This is not wisdom. It's impoverishment of the imagination.

This functional attitude even creeps into churches. The Mass, if we're not careful, can devolve into a delivery service for self-help, an arena for purely human activity instead of a participation in God's creative act, or the chance to manufacture cheap emotional catharsis. Hans Urs von Balthasar believes that our bereft imaginations have caused us to underestimate our Lord's action in the Holy Sacrifice. "Men have no inkling of what is occurring," he writes. "They simply walk on past it as over the dark pipes and drains that form the gruesome catacombs under our big cities. Up above the sun is beaming; peacocks fan their tails; young people frolic with glee, their light clothes puffed by the wind—and no one knows the price." Without poetic imagination, we cannot understand the Cross.

As a priest, this motivates me to get the details correct. I never know what ritual, gesture, or swing of the thurible will bring the poem to life.

Worship isn't for the sake of what we receive—although Christ does indeed offer infinite riches—it's an encounter with divine splendor. Worship that appeals to our senses and feeds imaginations is what allows us to behold that splendor accurately and adore God with wonder. Wonder, as Socrates teaches, is the beginning of wisdom. It's the secret ladder of beauty by which we ascend to eternal reality.

Christ wasn't kidding when He told us to become more like children.

✠ ✠ ✠

I offer upwards of ten Masses per week. Three on Sunday. By the third, I'm exhausted. Celebrating Mass takes concentration. It's work. It's work for me and for the faithful, the parents calming their children, the children resisting being calmed, all of us fighting daydreams, distraction, and anxieties.

This is as it should be. Earth is seeking Heaven. That's not easy.

More importantly, the Mass is Heaven seeking earth. No wonder we're red-eyed. I throw away so much strength trying to accomplish it all on my own when it's well and truly beyond my reach.

I finally understand St. Peter falling asleep in Gethsemane.

My goal in becoming Catholic was to finally wake up. Conversion was an act of love. Like all love, it wasn't easy. It was, however, immediately met by the love of a Mother. Maternal love, I am convinced, pries open the meaning of the Mass, and from there the meaning of our existence.

When you read a poem and the words stir your heart, an interior space is created. When you love someone, you behold with uncanny intimacy the truth and beauty of that person. When you love the Church, you gain deeper knowledge of her than if you merely know facts about her. In *The Science of the Cross*, Edith Stein writes, "Every genuine work of art is a symbol." She says it "comes from that infinite fullness of meaning into which every bit of human knowledge is projected to grasp something positive and speak of it. It does so in such a manner, in fact, that it mysteriously suggests the whole fullness of meaning, which for all human knowledge is inexhaustible."

> Fr. Hopkins puts it more idiosyncratically:
> All things counter, original, spare, strange;
> Whatever is fickle, freckled (who knows how?)
> With swift, slow; sweet, sour; adazzle, dim;
> He fathers-forth whose beauty is past change.

Hopkins is quite convinced that nothing is run-of-the-mill. All things have an inner life inscribed by Christ, participating in the beauty of the hidden God who fathers-forth creation. If there is beauty in this world, it's because there is One who is truly beautiful pouring Himself into it.

Aristotle gives a precise definition of *poetics*. It's the language of what *might be* and that *ought to be*. It's the language of hope. How clear is it, then, that poetry is the language of the Mass, through which we're reoriented toward Heaven.

Cardinal Newman writes in *Grammar of Assent*, "The heart is commonly reached, not through reason, but through the imagination. . . . Persons influence us, voices melt us, looks subdue us, deeds inflame us. Many a man will live and die upon a dogma, no man will be a martyr for a conclusion." Poetry reveals truth, as Cardinal

Ratzinger relates in a story in *Spirit of the Liturgy* about going to a concert with a friend:

> For me an unforgettable experience was the Bach concert that Leonard Bernstein conducted.... When the last note of one of the great Thomas-Kantor-Cantatas triumphantly faded away, we looked at each other spontaneously and right then we said: "Anyone who has heard this, knows that the faith is true."
>
> The music had such an extraordinary force of reality that we realized, no longer by deduction, but by the impact on our hearts, that it could not have originated from nothingness, but could only have come to be through the power of the Truth that became real in the composer's inspiration.

Through poetic beauty, the existence of God is revealed. Consider St. Henry Walpole, who was present for the martyrdom of St. Edmund Campion at Tyburn. The blood of the dying saint splattered his shirt. Walpole took this as a sign. He too became a priest, and then a martyr. He recorded his experience in a poem:

> Why do I use my paper, ink and pen
> And call my wits to counsel what to say?
> Such memories were made for mortal men;
> I speak of Saints whose names cannot decay.

Why write a poem? Why not mount a political insurrection against Queen Elizabeth? An editorial for the local newspaper? Because only poetry captures the heroism of martyrdom. Against the mighty government of England, a poem speaks a greater word. The poetic capacity to shine transcendent light on our daily lives is essential for our self-understanding. I cannot explain what I learned from a poem the way I might explain how to build a birdhouse, but certain truths we only encounter through analogy and mystery. The Mass isn't a lifeless construct—it's a living universal. Through it, God involves Himself in our lives with the utmost seriousness.

I'm always looking for the stillness beyond the flux. A good poem explains more, even, than the author himself intends. We can never fully explain an analogy, cannot presume to know everything about a poem. It's impossible. We live poetry and it grows in us. We don't merely attend the Mass. We don't merely appreciate its poetic beauty. We live it.

These are deep waters. Beauty is disorienting, offering no toehold, no niche to settle upon. There's a reason that the Psalmist cries out,

I have come into deep waters,
and the flood sweeps over me. (Ps. 69:2)

Abbé Henri Bremond compares a poem to swimming. It's not a controlled environment, but I don't want to dip my toe in and back away. When I entered the Church, I didn't set any boundaries. I'll try to walk on water, if that's what Christ asks. More likely, I'll plunge in and flounder around like St. Peter on his way to get breakfast. The point is, when I look out upon the breakers, I do so in expectation.

Our Lord cries from the Cross, "I thirst" (John 19:28, RSVCE). His thirst is for us, a desire with no end, satisfied only in the gift of His life for His beloved. A poem creates in us a sense of thirst, also. The soul seeks out its delight and beauty calls out to beauty. It would be a great tragedy to go through life ignorant of such depths, a true waste to be so afraid we never leave the shore.

In the first aphorism of *Either/Or*, Søren Kierkegaard writes, "What is a poet? An unhappy person who conceals profound anguish in his heart but whose lips are so formed that as sighs and cries pass over them, they sound like beautiful music." Beauty causes suffering because we desire more of it. The Mass isn't content to tinker with surface appearances. I've never expected it to make me into an "acceptable," moral, religious Christian. I expect it to make me into the image of Christ—a beautiful, terrifying, painful process. We don't always understand how God is remaking us. That's okay. Gerard Manley Hopkins didn't, either:

> I kiss my hand
> To the stars, lovely-asunder ...
> I greet him the days I meet him, and
>   bless when I understand.

We endeavor to meet God wherever He chooses to be found. Our task is to never stop looking. If nature is in flux, underneath is solid bedrock, a still point where God's time meets our time. The one immovable and eternal, the other all change and decay. T. S. Eliot writes,

> At the still point of the turning world.
>   Neither flesh nor fleshless;
> Neither from nor towards; at the still
>   point, there the dance is,
> But neither arrest nor movement.
>   And do not call it fixity,
> Where past and future are gathered.

The still point of the turning world. A spent rain cloud gray-hazed on the horizon, foliage dripping and shuddering. Pedaling a bicycle on a rusty bridge spanning the sun-glazed Mississippi many miles from home. A child pointing to a bird leaping from a nest and demanding that you, too, take heed. The miracle upon the altar.

Poetry isn't an intellectual curiosity. It's soil nurturing the seed of sainthood that grows to fruition in each human soul. A prelude for the life to come.

✠ ✠ ✠

The guest preachers at Oral Roberts were the kind of guys who wore snakeskin loafers and had exotic Australian accents. They were supremely confident. Pacing the stage, they held thousands of students in the palms of their rhetorical hands with anecdotes, shaky interpretive theories, and calls to culture war. For them, we would've run through a brick wall while speaking in tongues after having donated our meager tips from waiting tables all weekend. They snapped their fingers and the offertory basket filled.

At Yale, the guest bishops and priests were different. They oozed Waspish confidence and, even if less naturally gifted as speakers than their tent-revivalist brethren, more than made up for it with class, theological jargon, and the utter, complete, righteous conviction of their cause.

In turn, I imitated their patterns of speech. I picked up trendy phrases to deploy in practice homilies and took on a professorial drawl. We students were encouraged to speak prophetically and regularly address current social issues. It was made clear to us that we had a heavy responsibility to actively and decisively lead. I found myself forming quick but strong opinions. Half the time, they were wrong.

Secretly, I was concerned. I couldn't live like that, telling everyone what to do and pretending to an expertise I lacked. I still don't know how those preachers do it, spouting off such brazen opinions all the time, formulating their homilies down to aphoristic perfection. Looking to the future, I knew I couldn't be that kind of pastor. I didn't want to let my parishioners down, though, and fretted about how disappointing it would be for the faithful to endure my introversion and my tentative homilies. Would I ruin people's Sundays?

I thought I probably would. I think I probably have.

I don't think I would've consented to be ordained if I hadn't discovered the power of the sacraments. I'd been taught that I was the meaning-maker during worship. It was my task to lead, entertain, and dispense wisdom, but in fact, at Mass, the discovery of meaning is in the thing itself, in the Sacrament. As Church, our work is to unlock that meaning by means of language — metaphor, images, symbol — so that Christ's self-revelation will unfold. The point, though, is that Christ is there even if my homily isn't very good. His sacred language speaks louder than my halting words.

Returning to the chalice, for instance, Claudel calls it the Supreme Lily, a sign of creation rising from the center of history. My own chalice is decorated with metalwork depicting vines and leaves. When I place it on the altar, it flowers upward to unite dirt and sky, earth and Heaven, cradling Christ as Mary held Him on Christmas and again at the pieta. The chalice contains both life and death, the fullness of God's revelation. I may not be a natural public speaker, but I can hold a chalice.

The vines on the chalice are intriguing. Eden and Gethsemane are both gardens, places of beauty and rest. The reason I end up exhausted after some Masses is because I'm shrinking back to Eden when I should be lingering in Gethsemane. Falling backwards onto my own resources is exhausting and, ultimately, limiting.

Initially, it feels more difficult to trust God and give ourselves to Him than to rely on personal efforts, vanities, and spiritual consolations. This, perhaps, is why so much Catholic worship has become cluttered with human activity. But I've always found that, if I step back from myself and allow God to work, what is difficult at the outset reveals itself to be a source of grace-filled rest.

Sacramental grace is rooted in a garden beyond this world. The infusion of God's presence is caused only by itself. God alone is the Maker of grace. The bread, the wine, the priest, the people — we are entirely His.

✠ ✠ ✠

One theory of poetry is that language has developed into two kinds of speech—factual and metaphorical. In older times, this distinction didn't exist. Fact and metaphor were one. This is why, for instance, in Homer, the writing is simple but powerful. The *Iliad* begins, "Sing, O goddess, the anger of Achilles." This is a campfire tale of gods and battles, enchanted by flame and shadow, stated as simple fact. The divine and the human are mingled.

Not so in the modern world. Partly this is progress and partly regress. It's good that we've developed natural science and moved on from pantheism and capricious, false gods, but on the other hand we've excessively flattened everything to surface-level materialism. We can no longer find any place at all for Christ to animate this world. We're jaded and alienated, our language fractured and watery. When we speak, we describe objects as unrelated, even describing our own bodies as separate from our souls.

As a young teenager, I would sit up late into the night struggling to write poems or paint a masterpiece. I wanted to express myself and explain my strange, secret thoughts to my parents, friends, and even to myself. I couldn't do it. There I was, a privileged kid lying on his cushy bed, two parents, academically successful, but also anxious and dissatisfied. I felt something was wrong but couldn't express it. I didn't have the words. There were moments of clarity, transcendent beauty, but always the inevitable comedown. Walker Percy—a man who shouted as loud as he could that the problem with our language, the disappearing poetic, is a symptom of a deep crisis in the human soul—refers to it as "the spectacular miseries of reentry."

Fact is considered the most valuable language, but it's powerless to explain my own existence to myself. The good news is that metaphor allows us to speak again, and it does so while recognizing both divine immanence and transcendence. We don't have to retreat back to small gods in order to recover the poetic.

Metaphor is a door linking two different worlds. Natural and supernatural overlap and yet remain distinct.

Metaphor is access. It connects us to unknown realities through similarities and reveals that what I thought I comfortably knew is, in fact, the strange reality. I'm familiar with bread. You probably are, too. A normal everyday food item. It turns out that, at the Mass, bread becomes Sacrament.

Now I no longer know what to think about bread.

I thought I understood bread, the concept of it, the eating of it. I walk past thousands of breads, thin-sliced and plastic wrapped in the supermarket aisle. Is this prepackaged enriched bread a miracle? If so, is it possible the whole world is a miracle? The chance to encounter bread as it is in the Mass, although it raises questions, is enormously clarifying. I intuit more of what bread is supposed to be, what it *can* be. Not merely a delivery for nutrition, but our daily bread.

Those who assist at Mass engage in a deep mystery, one that through the poetic use of metaphor connects this world intimately to another — like connecting the scent to a flower, as C. S. Lewis might say. This mystery enchants our world, makes it far stranger, far more heroic, more meaningful. To embrace this mystery isn't religious obscurantism, it's clarity.

Metaphor is a revelation of the presence of Christ, fully human and fully God. He speaks and doors are thrown open. In Him, we are still ourselves — more ourselves than ever — but our individuality arises, paradoxically, from sharing His nature. He gives me Himself and I become myself. Same with a tree, the sun, the autumn. They all find their place in relation to Christ. Poetic perception is open to this deeper reality. Everyday language is not.

Metaphor, by holding the door open, becomes poetic memory. Every day, at the Mass, two realities are joined and I remember who I am.

A knowledge all its own, God's love is truth that must be expressed poetically. Yes, it's a fact that God loves you and me. A trustworthy fact as dependable as the rising of the sun. I always knew this. I hope you do, too. But I didn't *know* it. God's love is alive. It's the unnameable word that left me speechless the first time I experienced it at Mass, wrapping veins to bone and making a man out of mud.

The sun will rise tomorrow, yes. Picture, however, as Wallace Stevens does, a single bird basking in that sunlight with fire-fangled feathers. The sun isn't a fact to the bird. The sun is the glow in his feathers.

I've come to know the glow of God's love. It warms my skin and heats my soul. We live in a world of facts, but the world is ever so much more. As metaphor, it signifies eternal love. Somewhere in there, in the vastness of planets spinning through the vacuum and the smallness of crickets chirping from the pine-scented shadows, the muddle of human affairs and the clarity of the wind resting, breathing, bodiless against the womb of the earth, in the joining of earth to Heaven, there is sacramentality, the miracle of our Lord's abiding presence. Again, Wallace Stevens has found the right words: "He opens the door of his house / On flames."

There are constant attempts to turn the Blessed Sacrament into a commemoration, an empty ritual that gains meaning only from the intentions of the gathered community. What I want you to see is that this cannot be the case. If it was, the poetic would be annihilated, we would lose our connection to God, and I would probably regress into that frustrated teenager again.

Christ holds two worlds together into a single unity. As such, He creates all meaning. His Body and Blood are true food, at once physical and spiritual, a poem of such power that it re-fashions souls and bends the universe around itself until it's brand new.

The words are more simple than any Homeric epic, and yet accomplish infinitely more.

This is my body.

✠ ✠ ✠

To this day, I'm clueless why I was so motivated to become Catholic. All I know is that I was tired.

I was exhausted with justifying my personal beliefs. If I held a theological opinion, I had to prove it through my intellect. I couldn't rely on a tradition. If you've never had to fight to justify your faith, and by extension to justify the very drift and purpose of your existence, you might not realize how anxiety-riddled it is. It's like walking over a frozen sea on a skin of ice thinner than the width of a fingernail. Your breath hangs in the air. You're clinging by the fingertips. My own little world isn't enough. It never was.

The Church is her own lamp. She shines with the light of Christ Himself, a reality terrifying in its own way as I struggle to turn from my own shadow, but a divine terror full of excitement. Every once in a while, we need the suffering. I need to feel my hand tremble.

This is the way it happened. One day I wasn't interested in Catholicism. The next, I was. The process was immersive and tentative, but inevitable. I can't talk about it, and only shrug when asked why I became Catholic. The communion of saints sneaks up, surrounds you, and you know you've been placed under siege but willingly open the gates to your conqueror, so happy are you to surrender.

Describing it is similar to how I reach for profound ways of describing why poetry is so vital. I'm always dissatisfied with my explanations because I'm unable to share what it feels like to actually live it. The poem is the poem. The Church is the Church. An artifact of love.

So I sit in the sun that comes through the front windows of my house. Cut lilies in a clear vase on the mantel lift their faces to meet the light. They glow translucent. The lilies are sacred. They are metaphor. They are chalices.

Wallace Stevens once sat in the study of his Hartford home and similarly watched the sun. It filtered through a glass vase holding flowers. Then, a transfiguration:

The day itself
Is simplified.

He's like St. Peter on Mount Tabor. The air itself changes.

The light
In the room more like a snowy air,
Reflecting snow.

Toward the end of his life, poetry led Stevens into the Church, but years before, in that study, he's already swimming in clear water. The vase is an analogy holding two worlds in cohesion. He conceives a great desire for God. More even than the sun, God is a blinding brilliance, volcanic, and as the light glances off the curved glass it leaves Stevens snow-blind.

In my own journey, I carry an apocalyptic lamp, wavering between dark and light. God is in both. He's with me in doubt and fear, happiness and joy, heat and cold, triumph and sadness, life and death. Always, He is strong to save.

Like Dylan Thomas, I'm ready to plunge my hands in the snow and bring out whatever I can find.

Each morning, I'm a child seeing the sun for the first time. It's always new, always gesturing to the greater brightness of the life to come. In it, I glimpse the Host glowing translucent held by the fingers of Christ.

We cannot remain in His burning light. Not yet. We're still on our way, creatures of shadow and light, healed but still carrying about our fractures like our Lord in the Mass. Broken. Resurrected. Given.

In the Church, we navigate by light of dawn or fire of doomsday. Either way, I'm happy.

SIX
Desire Is Death

IN SEMINARY, I lurked in medieval glamor at Christ Church in downtown New Haven, where incense spills out the doors to where the homeless take refuge from the wind against the thick gray walls of the building. Christ Church has a rood screen and Lady Chapel. They chant evensong from the transept and host solemn, glittering liturgies. It's almost enough to make a person forget that Episcopalians are Protestant.

We High Church devotees wasted our afternoons at the Owl Shop on College Street, wrapped in Scottish tweed and smoke from our Egyptian cigarettes. Joe the tobacconist urged us to go see the Dominicans and get ourselves right, but we demurred. We glamorized Anglicanism, which we were convinced was already Catholic. Our version of the Church was free of papists and vulgarity. We stood for good taste, monarchy, and exquisite vestments. Romish nonsense. Penance, battered martyrs, the working class—those weren't for us. Far more important was sherry in the courtyard after prayers.

For an arrogant young aesthete, wisteria-shaded Anglicanism was pleasant. I loved my life and, to this day, occasionally pull my English-style surplice out of the sacristy closet and sigh. My desire was to worship in good taste, at a high altar and soundtracked by Tallis. There's much good in these, the antique traditions of the Church, beauty we desperately need in our age of poor passing facts. Older forms of worship may seem whimsical and quaint, undeserving of preservation in our modern, practical-minded world, but their oddball variance with office cubicles and superhighways is precisely their value. Modernity is obsessed with passing fads and fractured surfaces. In this context, gratuitous beauty is all the more precious. If the poetic disappears from the Church, it will disappear everywhere.

God, the inventor of apple pie, lemongrass, and rainbow trout, isn't the divinity of least common denominator, but flings creativity into the fields in every direction, into weeds and rocks. He slaughters the spotless Lamb and places the finest robe on His wayward son.

The mistake I made while in seminary was confusing good taste with the full depth of beauty. I didn't care for the ugly parts of Christianity—works of mercy, humility, hugging lepers, church potlucks. My concerns were elsewhere, mostly in researching boutique blends of incense.

Great art isn't always tasteful. It's a sacrifice of love—the disfigured face of Christ at the Passion is most beautiful of all—but I was reluctant to leave good taste behind for Catholicism. When I attended Masses, I was fascinated, but against my will. Some were beautiful. Most were banal. The music was poor, the priest hurried, the people inattentive. I glimpsed beauty, but often in spite of how the liturgies were celebrated. Holy Family Cathedral in Tulsa was lovely, but superficially it didn't measure up to Christ Church.

Then there was St. Francis de Sales in St Louis. The Masses offered there by the Institute of Christ the King are gorgeous. Years later, as a Catholic priest, I was invited to celebrate at the high altar. It was the most intimidating experience of my priesthood. I stumbled through the *Kyrie* and wracked my brain for the correct endings to the prayers. Meanwhile the servers serenely knelt on the step. They were born into the beauty as a gift. I was still practicing a threadbare art.

I suppose the Catholic Church has intimidated me for decades now. She's a ramshackle edifice somehow still breathing after two thousand years and, for the life of me, I cannot figure how she survives. Yet here I am, and don't regret for an instant my seedtime buried in the belly of this beast.

Back in New Haven, though, before I buried myself in the Church, my desires were at cross-purposes. One expression of beauty, Anglicanism, gave me great pleasure. The other, recklessly cast from Catholic altars, threatened to unmake me.

✠ ✠ ✠

"In the Trinity Term of 1929 I gave in," C. S. Lewis says, "and admitted that God was God, and knelt and prayed: perhaps, that night, the most dejected and reluctant convert in all England.... But who can duly adore that Love which will open the high gates to a prodigal who is brought in kicking, struggling, resentful, and darting his eyes in every direction for a chance of escape?"

I agree. It's surprising that God accepts a monstrous yet unfinished work of art such as my soul. Maybe my most serious objection to Catholicism is that it makes room for sinners like me, and worse yet—this is completely wild—has put me in a position of responsibility. Or maybe it's as simple as admitting that what we desire isn't what God desires. What we call beautiful is not what He calls beautiful.

I cannot remember a time I didn't love God. Even during the hormonal madness of teenage rebellion, even when I was refusing Sunday church and feeling betrayed by church leaders, I still loved God. That love was sincere, but I cannot help regretting that it was misshapen.

I loved God for His gifts. I was wildly interested in enforcing His side of our bargain. I didn't expect wealth and health—that kind of theology offended me—I had more sophisticated demands. My desires were unbroken happiness entirely on my terms, intellectual acumen, to be a beloved pastor who never fielded complaints, to never again feel loneliness or depression, to have every question answered to my satisfaction, to feel God in my soul in constant consolations, to ignore Him when I wanted and find Him when I needed. I wanted to fall asleep at night, even just one time, without dread of dark pinning me damply to the sheets. I wanted to stop fearing death.

None of this was forthcoming.

I thought God had failed. Recriminations were relentless because my love was conditional. I was chasing ways to satisfy my own compromised desire. I wanted everything. Serving God should've been met with rewards. But desire rightly ordered seeks God alone, to desire what He desires. I wasn't there yet—I still struggle mightily—and so, as Walker Percy might put it, my wants came howling down the Elysian Fields like a mistral.

Poet Ryan Wilson says poetry is the language that reorders desire, writing that it "allows for the commonality shared by individuals and experiences, the patterns that bind us together … poetry is and has been, from its beginnings, not about being cool or mysterious or sad or 'deep,' but about the health of the human spirit." As the poetry of the Mass continues to unfold for me, it gathers fragmented pieces of my life—unhealthy desires, ego, dissatisfaction, melancholy—and smooths the glassy shards back together. What I saw reflected in the mirror of Holy Mass was the first honest spiritual portrait I'd ever witnessed. I saw myself as God saw me.

To describe the portrait as surprising would be an understatement, which is why, today, I'm staggered and sheepish. I used to demand everything. Now I just want to learn to use the washing machine.

✠ ✠ ✠

"I am obscure as feeling is," says Pierre Reverdy. Poetic darkness intensifies as art shakes free from the constriction of logic, a process I found difficult. I hated the idea of resting in poetic darkness and not being in control. Openness to God's creativity is frightening in this way.

Logic, as an expression of control, had ruled my life. It was my own boutique logic which included everything I understood and impatiently disqualified everything else. I didn't understand the Church or the strange way Catholics take her strangeness for granted. Nor did I understand ragged bloodied martyrs, rosaries, transubstantiation, monstrances, or theology of the body.

It sounds like virtue, the relentless desire to hold opinions. In fact, it was a weakness that allowed me to dismiss anything outside the circle I'd drawn. Theological paradoxes and miracles were particularly galling. I obsessed over the problem of evil, predestination, and the authority of the Church.

I was obscure, laden with theological jargon. I thought word salad made me smart. In fact, it cut everything of value away—beauty, mystery, hope, tradition—all gone at the service of my pride. I chopped the poetic down and threw it in the furnace, the sacrificial fuel of personal desire. I thought I was a perfect theological computer creating an efficient set of beliefs. Instead, I burned up in the flame.

Logic must be held within poetic mystery. Shakespeare warns, "Desire is boundless and the act a slave to limit." The problem, as he sees it, is that we're perpetually unsatisfied when we get what we want, but are capable of wanting absolutely everything. Desire is monstrous. We cannot logically solve the conundrum. We can only address it poetically. More specifically, God has to address it poetically by reshaping us to desire Him alone. This meant I had to give up my sense of entitlement and need to control.

So often, we desire wrongly. Money, fame, reputation, our enemies ground into dust, whatever. Goodness, at times all I've wanted is the respect of my peers and for my infant child to stop screaming at midnight. Are these desires misguided? They aren't unreasonable, but perhaps misguided in the sense that they relate purely to my own ego and comfort.

Disordered desires cause unhappiness, but our never-dying, post-Eden fever dream is that one more wish granted will be the golden ticket back into the garden. It never is — after sin, we can't go back again — so the Mass drags us from Eden and toward the completely radical, Christian hope of the New Jerusalem. In the same way that reading a poem leaves you a different person than when you began, the Mass is transformational. The liturgy kills unhealthy desire only to bring us out of the tomb with the invitation to pick up the heaviest cross possible and carry it as far as we can. In doing so, we unite our desire, like Christ does, with the will of the Father. Our endless desire is met by His endless desire. Thus, as Wallace Stevens writes, does this dark and poetic love recreate:

> Here is an eye. And here are, one by one,
> The lashes of that eye and its white lid.
> Here is the cheek on which the lid declined,
> And finger after finger, here, the hand,
> The genius of that cheek. Here are the lips,
> The bundle of the body and her feet.

At times, as in the case of the baby screaming me awake when I have a morning meeting, it quite literally feels like torture to sacrifice our personal desire to God, to live the life He's given to each one of us. Actually, it's the stuff of heroic poetry. Even the crying infant is but the suffering of fatherhood.

The greatness of poetry isn't fulfillment of selfish desire, those fragmentary stilted wishes we conceive in jealousy and ego. The greatness of poetry is to make sacred a forest, a sunrise, a lifelong marriage, a man and his children, winter snow—revelations of grace within the commonplace. These moments of beauty bend around the gravitational pull of the Mass, the weight of love drawing the faithful week after week, year after year, to a poetry that grows and mends our tired souls and, to those who are patient and humble, reveals God.

I suppose I'd been Catholic for a few years already when it dawned on me that God had authored the cosmos as sacred poem before personally entering into it. The *Logos* is poetic logic enthroned high above my own, scrawny ideas. Jacques Maritain says, "The logical sense has been digested, so to speak by the poetic sense, it has been broken up, dislocated." This is why "the poetic sense alone gleams in the dark."

Through pride and disordered desire, my logic was blinded. The only path forward has been the Mass. As poetic knowledge, liturgy is purgative, stripping away flaws to reveal the perfect written line of what my life can become, a divine word that hides and reveals, uncovering depths beyond reckoning. From the lips of God, a kiss from the Beloved. Christ is the fulfillment of desire and fullness of logic, walking the valley of the shadow of death with us every step of the way.

✠ ✠ ✠

The times I've returned to Yale, the elm-shaded courtyards were haunted. The buildings were the same, but my friends were no longer there. It's been the same experience every time I've left a city. The city's face turns away.

Most of the time, I feel vaguely as though I'm abandoning one place for another. I worry about the past I've left behind, that I'm still leaving behind. I miss old friends, the white beaches where I gave my toddlers slices of pepperoni pizza from the box, the house where my children were born in the bedroom, the basement club in Boston where my favorite band played guitars so loud my ears hurt and afterward we drank martinis near the Common. It's a heartache to have known those places, as if desire has bent back on itself, circled round, elevated, expanded to hold my days within her grasp and yet still demands more. One moment I'm invincible, the next confused and hurt that time refuses to linger. Our toddler eagerly fumbles through a story and I'm nostalgic even while I laugh and tussle his hair. I'm sad when the turntable soundtracks a golden heat-soaked St. Louis night while children play at my feet. I play Debussy at the piano in the darkened living room and am bereft, sad when the cappuccino cup is empty, sad to transfer parishes as a pastor. These wounds never heal, but I'm happy to have them. My heart is worn to ash, but only because a fire burns.

Dylan Thomas puts it magnificently in "Fern Hill":

Time held me green and dying
Though I sang in my chains like the sea.

Identity and desire are life and death questions. That which we desire is what we give our hearts to, and we take on the identity of our loves. During seminary, I secretly began to love the Mass. I still filtered my love through my fondness for Anglicanism, but already felt a pulling away. It made me sad to know that I probably wouldn't die an Anglican. One more city left behind. I couldn't acknowledge the departure, yet, because my personal desire kept pulling me toward Anglicanism. I was becoming convinced the Catholic Church is the Church, but didn't *want* to be Catholic.

I needed God to destroy me.

All we leave behind is devoured by time, so it's only a question of how the destroyer arrives. I can clutch my pearls and, soon enough, find that desire has ruined me. Or I can give my desire to God as a willing sacrifice.

Because it's an act of sacrificial love, poetry is destructive. Paul Claudel calls it movement. Bachelard a change. I think it's carrying a cross. The point is, poetics unmakes and then makes. The Mass, in particular, is the complete annihilation of our Lord on the Cross. Coupled with His perfect love, the destruction becomes sacrifice, the science of spiritual rebirth, the great engine by which a soul is transfigured. From the sacrifice an earthquake erupts that pulls down the temple of man. Before it, bread and wine cannot stand. The human heart is torn like tissue paper so Christ can enter.

What happens when such dangerous beauty gets inside us? And we consume the Eucharist willingly, casually! It's a death. Not a figurative death but a real, genuine reckoning. If we would become great art, we cannot avoid the sacrifice, but in the harrowing Christ destroys the power of sin to determine our desires. We are raised from the dead having taken on His image.

It's a choice we must repeatedly make, this choice for God. He makes us new creations and we take on His form, but as Claudel warns, "Form is not the result of cutting out a pattern once and for all, but the product of a constant operation which maintains it." The Mass, in its ancient poetic form, describes infinite movement and unceasing creative power, from complete alienation into child of the Kingdom, from below a worm to greater heights than the seraph.

☩ ☩ ☩

How is a poem made? The author has an idea, arising from an observation of, say, a leaf dying on a branch, a hummingbird's clumsy enthusiasm, children wobbling on bicycles back and forth on the sidewalk. The best poems are about everyday experiences. The poet observes, excavates, pokes, and prods. Everyday objects and experiences are plowed under the soil into a crucible. Then, as Hopkins writes, they buckle.

Watching a hawk fly, he exclaims, "The fire that breaks from thee then, a billion / Times told lovelier, more dangerous, O my chevalier!" Hopkins turns the soil, "and blue-bleak embers, ah my dear, / Fall, gall themselves, and gash gold-vermilion." He explores interior landscapes and, wherever his poetic gaze drifts, Christ outshines even the brightest star.

Hopkins isn't naïve. Beauty is sacrifice, not the hunt and capture of personal desires. The entire cosmos, one great, magnificent act of beautiful creativity, is a sacrifice of love from Christ.

The Host outshines the cosmos and yet the priest pries it open, breaks it like a twig in the hands of a toddler. Watch and you'll observe him amputate a small particle and mingle it into the bloody chalice. The desire of our Lord is given to the Father. It is Christ in Gethsemane praying, "Not my will but yours be done" (Luke 22:42). Blood beads from His skin like anointing oil under the stones of an olive press. Crushed under the weight of the Cross, only in such a manner is glory achieved. In the unification of desire, that of the Son with His Father, we are saved. What a beautiful and tragic scene. The misplaced desire of one garden, Eden, healed in another garden. The mingling of Host with Precious Blood signifies that the healing has taken place. It was our misplaced desire that fractured Christ, but His healing of desire that reunites soul and body in the reality of the Resurrection.

It's all sacrifice. We take our place on the altar alongside our Lord to be broken. We are victims of love, mended by sacrifice. This is the mystery of poetry. If you dig deep enough, it's all gold.

When you behold the eucharistic Host, does it shine?

✠ ✠ ✠

It's said that St. Wenceslaus, even though a king, removed his shoes and personally crushed grapes to make sacramental wine. It's a simple drink, wine—nothing more than a few ingredients. Bread is also a plain food. Both are transubstantiated into Christ.

Imagine placing your own simple offering on the altar alongside the bread and wine—washed dishes and folded laundry, kids dropped off to soccer practice, taxes dutifully paid, kindness given away, the harsh word not said. These represent the sacrifice of desires, the chores and obligations we fulfill even though we'd prefer to spend our days in other pursuits. These gifts are incense crushed to powder and burned to release fragrance. God transforms every last one into perfume.

Maybe it's appropriate that every year I retreat into wine country for spiritual struggle. If anything, I'm a grape that must be crushed so it can release the sunshine it has been gifted.

The poet Kay Ryan says, "If we are not compelled to submit in some way to a poem it cannot change us." This has been my experience also. She goes on: "We're converts here, or we've quit." Again, yes. We must fully abandon ourselves to the Mass or better not participate at all.

St. Augustine, in his *Confessions*, tells how disordered desires made him soul-sick, covering him like a fleshy garment he couldn't shake. He knew it was either his desires or God's, not both, but it took a long time to choose. He would sit in the garden and brood. "I was troubled in spirit," he recalls, "most vehemently indignant that I entered not into Thy will and covenant, O my God, which all my bones cried out unto me to enter, and praised it to the skies. And therein we enter not by ships, or chariots, or feet, no, move not so far as I had come from the house to that place where we were sitting."

Søren Kierkegaard had a similar experience; "Let us look as how they fling themselves from one pleasure to another: their password is variation ... they desire many different things, and he who wants in these circumstances is not only innerly dispersed, but also divided."

I, like Augustine and Kierkegaard and all of you, have felt divided, one part eager to enter under the roof of our Lord and the other seeking excuses to run away. This is why I was mystified by the Mass for many years.

By turn, it was heart-stoppingly beautiful and exquisitely boring. I loved plainchant in its natural setting, a music never meant for the concert hall but to be sung with aching devotion in a church. The singing floated down from the choir loft, pure as ivory, but straining against the hauntingly serene melody. Just underneath the surface pulsed a heartbeat of desire, brimming with the blood and marrow of the saints.

The sacredness of the liturgy verged on crushing the priest beneath its weight. The prayers popped like static in my ear. I ran out of concentration, thoughts slovenly wandering to dreams of bacon and eggs. I was very much out of place. I still experience jarring displacement until I remember to rest in God's grace.

There was some lingering mystery that whispered secrets just out of earshot. As we walked home after one of those early Masses, I marveled to a friend that it felt like coming unstuck in time. Subsequently, I've witnessed newcomers wander out of Masses I've offered at Epiphany in similar confusion. One poor soul clutched her temples and complained how completely lost she felt.

Looking back, my passions had been formed toward easy entertainment, eager for something to consume. I wanted something to *do*. Both in life and in worship I became physically uneasy if I wasn't productively employed in some activity. Gradually, I stopped behaving so frantically and internalized the outward form of the

Mass. Its inward meaning unfolded—a metaphysical change, desire transfigured by beauty.

Beauty can tear apart an unwary aspirant. So, too, can the Mass, which destroys and recreates. There's a sense of loss that the beauty of the Mass slips away, an unrepeatable moment in a lifetime condemned to picking up shards of beauty that reflect the heavens, but only if we hold them very still and just so. Eventually, every hand trembles.

The Mass is the greatest of all art, and it requires the most from us. We approach with disordered affections and malformed sensibilities only to be confronted by unyielding beauty, beauty so chaste that, in order to approach it, it must first remake us.

My simultaneous attraction and repulsion to the Mass made it painfully clear I wasn't ready, didn't really know God the way I thought I did, neither His beauty nor goodness, maybe not even His love. I could write a five-thousand-word term paper on a theological topic, was confident in my vocation to be a pastor, but nevertheless sat outside the house, divided.

The Mass is desire. If other desires displace it, we become alienated from ourselves. Disordered desire eventually gains mastery over us. This was my problem. It still is my problem, addiction to sin and loss of self. Gaining ourselves back is a battle. This is what Augustine struggled with and what I struggle with. It's what we all struggle with. But struggle we must, otherwise all desire eventually dies and life loses joy.

Rumor has it that religion is passionless. Sinners delight in sensual groves while Catholics kneel in soggy puritan stoicism, gazing upon technicolor illustrations of baby angels. Religion is supposedly safe, a divine insurance racket to guarantee an eternal retirement. It turns out, however, that outside the Church the desires we cling to so stubbornly wither. Modernity, or whatever jumble of pick-your-own poison from the options of casual sex, productivity and career, gross consumerism, and anesthetizing comfort-seeking, has dehumanized us. Pop culture crafts a world of secret loneliness, deliberate childlessness, and desperate attempts by Hollywood to make us feel again, feel anything, through ever-increasing imitations of eroticism on screen. Desire has devolved to eat-pray-loving around the world, only to return home and realize we're still stuck with ourselves.

The Mass is the height of desire. Here, sensible beauty directs us to properly ordered passion—desire for God—which unites our particular desires with universal love, baptizing them into a whole new order of magnitude and power. Catholicism isn't Puritanism. It's a society dedicated to guarding and stoking the embers of desire, to love and love deeply.

In the *Divine Comedy*, Dante explores desire, which is out of control and has ruined his life. He writes his poetry in exile, barred from returning to his home city of Florence and dreaming about a girl named Beatrice he'd seen once, many years before.

The cure isn't leaving desire behind, but rather, learning to desire rightly. To get there, Dante must take a journey. He begins on a downward trajectory, sinking into Hell to witness the chaos there, a necessary movement because he's in despair. His disordered desires have left him lost. To find himself, he witnesses the consequences of unresolved desire, crawls through Purgatory, and only then emerges into Paradise. His journey is the healing of desire.

Desire without a proper object is useless. For want of direction it exhausts itself, eats us up, or moderates into vague platitudes, motivational posters plastered on the walls of a cubicle. It isn't enough to desire a bland vision of world peace. Simply imagining a generic utopian world isn't a stand-in for real love. This is why pop culture is so boring. It's an ersatz, abstract idea that fails to capture the real thing.

Nietzsche, keen to reintroduce desire into sterile modernity, claims, "Christianity gave Eros poison to drink." He believes — like so many others — that recovering passion requires rejecting the Church. He senses the problem but has the solution backwards. The Church is actually the only place where desire is alive.

Pope Benedict XVI, writing about twisted desires in the ancient world that resulted in the degradation of women, says that Israelite religion "declared war on a warped and destructive form of [eros], because this counterfeit divinization of eros actually strips it of its dignity and dehumanizes it." He goes on: "Eros needs to be disciplined and purified if it is to provide not just fleeting pleasure, but a certain foretaste of the pinnacle of our existence, of that beatitude for which our whole being yearns."

Desire is renunciation. We cannot long for everything under the sun. Renunciation isn't limitation, as Benedict explains; "it is part of love's growth towards higher levels and inward purification that it now seeks to become definitive, and it does so in a twofold sense: both in the sense of exclusivity (this particular person alone) and in the sense of being 'for ever.'"

If desire is an arrow, it must eventually strike home.

Beatrice isn't written into the *Divine Comedy* out of sentimentality. She's there because Dante needs to come to grips with desire. The nebulous concept of passion isn't what motivates his journey. Rather, it's Beatrice, a specific woman with her own particular way of walking down the street. Even though he must learn to desire her with chastity, for Dante she's the muse through whom universal love reveals itself. By healing his passions, he regains all he has lost.

God doesn't save us from our sins by fiat. He chose to take on flesh as a specific person inhabiting a life all His own. He is Emmanuel, God with us. Not content with abstract love, our Lord gets dirty in the mud of a Bethlehem stable, and pries open a wound in His side. This isn't the way it had to be for our salvation, but it's the way God chose. His desire is so intense that it incarnated. He wants to love us personally.

Our desire, properly ordered, has the same force. We bury ourselves in the waters of Baptism, consent to the bond of marriage, and lay down our lives in the grinding, wearying martyrdom of parenthood. I would do anything for my children, just like my father would do anything for me. Desire is a seed that falls to the earth and dies for a beloved so it can flower. The bud bursts open for Dante as he purifies and follows desire into heavenly spheres.

Real love, real desire, begins at the personal level. Every day, I become Dante. I hug my sticky-faced kids and laugh when the toddler interrupts my reading by quacking like a duck behind my chair, clean the pots and pans stuck with burnt eggs, read bedtime stories when my throat is hoarse and all I want is to crawl into bed and watch the game on television. I learn to love with my crooked heart, sink to the floor on aching middle-aged knees to play match game. I've been turning off lights in empty rooms of our house for the last twenty years. It would be easier, far easier, to love humanity as a generic idea, but love specific persons we must. Desire only finds the path forward by loving real, actual people who are imperfect.

It's easier to love the idea of the Mass than actually join Christ in offering a specific, thoughtful sacrifice, a personal laying down of desire. This hurts, but nothing replaces actually being there. Good intentions are not enough; appreciating the Mass is not enough. What's required is that God's very real desire would be met by our very real desire.

If it's tempting to love in the abstract, at the opposite extreme it's also tempting to halt with the love of a specific person or object, as if that's the limit. It can be terrifying to open up to the God who desires us without end, but there are no outer limits on virtues because, by their nature, they participate in God's infinite virtue. They cannot be limited without being neutered.

In *Paradiso*, Beatrice describes love as an arrow shot to Heaven. Its true essence escapes the imagination. Love is eternal, wild, and unbounded. Our souls must be enlarged through the purification of desire if we are to stand even the smallest, faintest glimmer. When Dante sees the divine reflected in the eyes of Beatrice, he finally follows that arrow.

Robert Royal remarks that "Dante does something that no other medieval troubadour ever thought to do. For all the talk in love poetry about seeing God in the beloved's eyes, no one had previously imagined that it might be possible to turn from the reflection in those pupils and look upon the source of that light itself." Beatrice isn't jealous. She wants Dante to desire God more than her:

> And all my love was so absorbed in Him,
> that in oblivion Beatrice was eclipsed.
> Not this displeased her; but she smiled at it ...

Royal says that Dante "will fulfill his relationship to her and transcend it without abandoning her: Heaven permits many such paradoxes, the basis of all of them being that as we draw closer to the primal unity, the multiplicity of the cosmos becomes truer also, truer in that both we and our relationships with each other become more authentic."

Dante realizes he is seeing virtue itself instead of its appearances. His desire has followed the natural order of rooting itself first in sensible objects, in Beatrice as a real person to be loved chastely, and now he peers more universally into the pure essences underlying existence:

> The circles corporal are wide and narrow
> According to the more or less of virtue
> Which is distributed through all their parts.

In the introduction to his translation of the *Divine Comedy*, Anthony Esolen says, "To love a human being is also to love the body. To love the body is to love the small, the local, the particular. It is to love those things enjoyed by that body—even to love Florence, or to use Burke's phrase, the small platoon into which one was born. It is to love Bag End and the beer from a particularly good harvest."

The Mass makes us love it, the particularity of it, the unique shade of how we arrive and hear the missional call to a first light, the day of Creation. If at first it seems an elegy for a deceased Savior as the language runs from the altar, it becomes more and more clear that the sacrifice is, in fact, a signifier that through Christ we are more alive than ever. Each precious soul, laid down as sacrifice, doesn't dribble out into wan loss of self and desire but, rather, becomes all muscle and bone, all resurrected grace concentrated on raising the living from the dying. Fresh and sweet, the poetic language flies like echo to source, its body a living form, a fountain of memory and imagination.

Through a particular, individual Mass, God speaks all of time into existence. He knits you and me, we injured Adams and Eves, into a communion of saints.

Cradled within this paradox, I learned to love. My unhealthy desires were broken against the rock of God's desire. No longer am I fixated on grand, abstract ideas, theological arguments, and the vague dehumanized disquietude in my soul. I adore the particularities of the Mass, its physicality, its enchanted imagination, the personalities of different parishes, each parishioner, quirky and idiosyncratic, the guy who rushes to say amen before everyone else, the woman who refuses to say the *Agnus Dei* in Latin with everyone else, the antiphons turning like a golden spiral, each one heralding a new season that discovers me as a pilgrim, a specific aspirant in a specific place on the journey. There, at morning Mass, rubbing sleep from my eyes, I've learned to love the good and beautiful things in this world, and the more I love them the more I love God.

From the particular to the universal, desire expands the soul. My first instinct was to reject the Mass or adapt it to my own wants. I found it threatening and stilted, but kept returning because desire had gotten hold of me. The little things I loved about it, as challenging as they were, eventually converted me to the weightier truths. This is the order, each following our Beatrice and practicing love right where we are. In doing so, we proceed to a brightening vision of God. We rise up and walk.

If I gaze into the night sky as Dante's rose unfolds petals overhead, and with the eye of a lover I see beyond the stars to the saints in a slow dance around the Source of all Being, I would perhaps feel the gravity of desire as it circles ever more tightly into the unity of love. As Dante famously concludes,

> But already my desire and my will
> were being turned like a wheel, all at one speed,
> by the Love which moves the sun and the other stars.
> Perhaps you feel it already.

✠ ✠ ✠

For years, I wondered if the Mass was enough. I desired to give myself to a noble cause to make my existence meaningful. We dream about power, wealth, respect, and accomplishments. Personally, I've wanted at various times to be a novelist, poet, professional basketball player, urban hipster, world-weary traveler, or Ivy League snob. I've dreamed of attending a public high school, of having a nose without a bump in it, of riding my bicycle up Mont Ventoux, of tending bar on a tropical island, of feeling normal. What I ended up with is a terrible novel, no talent as a poet, sleepless crying babies, and a thousand tiny waxy fingerprints on the living room window by the chess set.

I couldn't be happier.

Desires change. The poem I thought I was writing turns out to be entirely different. This reformation is the effect of graces dispensed at the Mass. I'd already chased all manner of dead ends and was finally left, dejected, on the porch of the Church with nowhere else to turn with all those itchy, unfulfilled desires that crawled under my skin.

I heard God's voice calling out and waked to His will because He welcomes me every day into His story, greatly desiring, in fact, that I be there. And it's me, specifically, that He wants. And it's you, too. God doesn't pursue the vague idea of a Catholic. He isn't after cookie-cutter, magazine-glossy religious automatons. He wants me to be me, more myself every day. He pours Himself out in desire—we see it in every aspect of the Mass—so I can be the best version of myself. Every day I ascend to the altar and into endless possibility, right there at the dawn of the eighth day of creation.

Pierre-Jean Jouve writes, "Poetry is a soul inaugurating a form." I wonder what God is shaping me into? My desires are changed but more deeply felt. The old are discarded as not enough. Whatever I'm up to these days—I'm still trying to write but am less interested in actively pursuing snobbishness—I unite with the desire to love ardently, live poetically, and so put on the wedding garment of Christ. He purifies desire a thousandfold, magnified into a love for life so intense it's almost painful.

God has placed eternity in our hearts and nothing will satisfy but Him. Unrequited, this mismatched love causes suffering and unhappiness, because in denying God we deny our deepest desire and thus our own selves.

St. Bonaventure says to search out the God of fire, even if the quest requires the last drop of blood we have, sacrificed for the Beloved. "He who loves this death can see God," he writes; "therefore let us die and step into the darkness, let us put on silence with its cares, and concupiscences and phantasms; let us pass over together with Christ Crucified from this world to the Father, that, by showing us the Father, we may say with Philip: It suffices for us."

SEVEN
Holding Open Doors

IN 1902, THE French government dissolved over ten thousand Catholic schools along with many monasteries. This included the Grande Chartreuse, where the local peasants erected burning barricades to keep the army from enforcing the order. The soldiers responded by taking axes to the monastery gates. The monks processed out the door singing, flanked by rows of weeping Catholics.

A doorway is a transition, a way in or out. Families bless the doorways to their homes with Epiphany chalk to guard their entrances and departures. Before an infant is baptized, the family gathers on the church porch outside the nave, only making their way through the door after the priest makes the Sign of the Cross on the infant's forehead. A new bishop is required to beat the door of his cathedral open with his crosier.

A doorway is humbling. It might be a sign of defeat, a forced exit, a plea to God for protection, or a request for entry into the communion of saints. Christ speaks of the narrowness of doors, the cost they exact for passage. It's as if each symbolic doorway of our lives, the obstacles we must pass through in order to make progress, possesses a secret password. The password is always "humility."

The Habsburg burial tradition offers a touching example of doors and Christian humility. The Habsburgs were known as the "first family of Christendom" and had enormous wealth and political influence in Europe for many centuries. They were emperors and kings, patrons of the arts, and above all, Catholics.

When the Habsburg emperors in the Austrian Empire were buried, the grand chamberlain of the royal court would seek entrance for the casket into the Capuchin friary in Vienna which held the crypt for the imperial family. Standing outside, the grand chamberlain knocked with a silver cane on the door. From inside, the Capuchin porter asked, "Who is there?" The grand chamberlain proclaimed the name and titles of the deceased man: "I am … Emperor of Austria, Apostolic King of Hungary, King of Bohemia, Dalmatia, Croatia." The porter refused to open the door, saying, "I do not know you."

The Grand Chamberlain knocked a second time with the same result: "I do not know you."

He knocked a third time. When asked, "Who is there?" the Grand Chamberlain simply said, "I am … a poor mortal and a sinner."

To this, the Capuchin friar opened the door with the words, "Come in."

Being alive entails damage, fragmentation. We suffer merely by existing. Blame our pride, the relentless ego we all seem to have that pushes us out the door into the night, tearing us from home, from Eden and into the desert. We try to get back in by pounding away at the door, proclaiming that we deserve it. The door remains closed.

Wandering on the outside produces a kaleidoscopic effect, our actions and motivations shattered to pieces with no coherent whole, no firm identity. It's unfortunate, then, that arrogance is our primordial flaw. Pride is the sin that motivates all our other sins and it keeps us from asking for forgiveness. Perhaps this is why our spiritual journeys are all so difficult. Maybe it's why the Mass feels like being squeezed through the eye of a needle.

Home, to me, is hearth fire, children's art tacked to the walls, a Sigur Rós album on the turntable, and a disheveled pile of novels on the table. The older I become, the more determined I am when walking out the door each morning to arrive back home in the evening. I'm not interested in staying out late. I simply want to tie on my dressing gown and have a drink in my threadbare red chair while children play at my feet.

Searching for home put the first dent in my ego when I finally admitted I was powerless to find it and that even my current domestic bliss can only be temporary. The children will empty-nest me, and at best, we're a wandering tribe no matter how imposing the wrought-iron door of our home seems to be. Our shelter is God alone. The Mass is a room, a poetic stanza unfolding a space in which we dwell, a resonance that calls forth beauty and drapes us under the shadow of God's wing. Poetic beauty, in general, is a shelter carved out by artists from their love, a tabernacle within which we rest. Ultimately, though, Christ is the Gate by which all beauty travels.

We can't huddle even in this poetic shelter forever. This is why beauty makes us homesick. Through it we participate in divine love but, as St. Peter learned, we can't build a permanent dwelling in the shadow of the Transfiguration. The Mass, nevertheless, is a sacramental participation in our true home. We're really there. This is why it's the source of poetry, and why, if we're ever to find our place in this world, the Mass is essential. It not only draws us into the heavenly mansion, but also shelters us in the doorway as we travel through life.

Lift up your heads, O gates!
and be lifted up, O ancient doors!
that the King of glory may come in. (Ps. 24:7)

✠ ✠ ✠

Words are stubborn. It takes time to find the right one sufficient to the moment. Poetry sinks roots, searching into veined crevices of the earth, discovering there under our feet some maternal heartbeat hardly noticed above, resurrecting ancient riverbeds, fossils, the joys of a thousand summers. It's von Balthasar's heart of the world. Our most sacrificial and beautiful loves are buried deep, particularly the Passion of our Lord, because the reality is too difficult to face. He says, "This must be so. And it must be hidden, men have no inkling of what is occurring. They simply walk on past it as over the dark pipes and drains that form the gruesome catacombs under our big cities. Up above the sun is beaming; peacocks fan their tails; young people frolic with glee, their light clothes puffed by the wind—and no one knows the price."

My pride makes me impatient with verbal digging. Only humility and honesty attain self-knowledge and, further, uncover the right word to name reality. Ego has made me hasty in spiritual life, nurturing relationships, and accurate self-knowledge. It took me far too long to humble my thoughts and words, allow God to reveal my flaws, and not show off with how much I knew. What a challenge it is to wait on the poetry, sink to the depths with Christ, and feel the cost of love.

Overcoming ego is a monstrous task. An examen is like a tolling bell rocking in the cradle between destruction and creation. Old church bells, blessed and given names, call us into the Mass and our own spiritual death.

Sin has made our modern era old and tired. We lack courage to risk the creativity of poetry, preferring surface-level interactions, consumerism, and comfort. We can't be bothered to rise to the challenge of even attending Mass, let alone responding authentically to the voice of God calling us to lay down our lives and follow Him. It isn't that we've rejected God. We don't even care, and won't be bothered to formulate the words to describe why we don't care. No justification is needed. Just lazy mediocrity.

Mankind used to be more optimistic, more aware of our connectedness to the world, and thoughtful about how God interacts with creation. Language was more poetic, every word tightly linked to a concrete idea. A tree was *this* tree. This oak. A specific oak I know and love, grace lurking within like sap oozing through the bark.

Homer's stories, for instance, are more than they appear. He doesn't write inner dialogue or describe emotion. He doesn't theologize or rhapsodize. The story is simple yet pregnant with meaning. It's poetic.

In our allegedly sophisticated modern era, words are empty and stripped. We speak functionally to communicate facts. These facts, however, aren't necessarily connected to reality the way we think they are. They're gray lifeless things, these facts we're so proud to know. They describe appearances but never get to the full truth.

I worry this verbal incompleteness has seeped into the Mass. As sacred language, the liturgy loses its poetic, sacramental character when treated as functional. It's a dangerous idea that we attend Mass in order to benefit somehow—as if we deserve entertainment, spiritual consolations, emotional highs, or clever advice—and if practical applications are missing then the Mass has failed.

The truth is, the Mass isn't practical. Grace isn't self-help. We don't always extract noticeable benefits. Better to think of it the other way around. Mass puts something into us by battering our hearts to smithereens. It crams grace into us whether we have an inkling of what that means or otherwise. It's really not up to you or me how it happens or what we feel about it. Tidal waves of grace descend to drown us even as we yawn.

How many Catholics are brimming with the Holy Spirit and hardly notice? We're walking sonnets and don't know it—Shakespeares who refuse to write.

Contending for beauty in the Mass doesn't make you rigid, or even especially traditionalist. It means you love beauty, that you love God very much and want to speak His language. His Word sparkles with grace, creative of souls, stars, and heavenly realms. We don't read worship as a fact. We live it as hope.

The Mass is the height of poetry, not overly precious or artificial but, rather, the authentic voice of the High Priest, the worded bond of love between Son and Father. Composed at the dramatic peak of tightly controlled passion, forged in Gethsemane, joined by the communion of saints and the plenitude of human feeling, it's how God speaks us into the new creation. Christ is poet and bridge, offering not a description of some thing, an object or idea, as if the meaning and substance of worship is a practical takeaway. Mass is the thing itself—the widow's mite, last meal, spear to the heart, rib torn from your side. It's blood and water, a stone manger scraped bare of wheat.

During my life, I've been so arrogantly needy to exercise the illusion of control that my worldview at times was entirely intellectual. I had dearly held beliefs I would argue until blue in the face. I had commitments. Couldn't back down. Admitting boundaries to my intellect brought unease, so I pretended that, given enough time, I would know absolutely everything—a fragmenting lie in the center of who I was.

It goes back to the division of poetry from superficial communication. I was shallow even while I thought I was deep, intellectual but unable to recognize knowledge because true knowledge is a unified, poetic mode of thinking. This is how pride propels us out the gate of Eden. Left behind is the tree of knowledge. In claiming ownership of it, we lost it.

Humility, on the other hand, leads to innocence and wisdom. When knowledge is innocent, the world scoffs and calls it childish, but innocent knowledge is superior, the memory of a world of possibility. Possibility is a poetic mode of language, if you recall, that puts us into a state of emergence.

The language of the Mass is innocent and trusting, so much so that it seems naïve. Perhaps you even rush to qualify it when you describe it to a non-Catholic. But we cannot escape the reality that we really believe there is a God who accepts us and grants mercy. The priest really believes God is listening, the bread becomes Christ, and angels are in the room. The simple words of Christ are creative act. Reality is transfigured, and you and I, trusting children holding our Mother's hand, step through the door.

Wonder, as Socrates teaches, is the beginning of wisdom. Cynicism, fake sophistication, and irony prevent understanding of reality because cynical people are unduly dismissive. They see the Mass and can only pity those who believe and, in doing so, their ego causes them to miss the miracle.

Perhaps the real challenge with innocence is that it makes us vulnerable. With all the tragedy, arguing, and grasping selfishness out there, it seems smarter to defend ourselves from the world rather than to welcome it with open arms. My arrogance is a coping mechanism for my hesitation to be wounded and, more than anything, it's a salve for my nagging self-consciousness. I'd rather be roasted over an open flame than speak a single sentence out loud I haven't already mentally contemplated at length. I don't want to give the toast at the party. My jokes are awkward. No one laughs. I preach with a full text as a safety blanket, and without a manuscript I white-knuckle the ambo. I don't want to act in a play, dance at a wedding, or pray a spontaneous prayer. It all seems so *embarrassing*.

I don't mind being the center of attention, but I want to be in control. If more than six people will be at a dinner and I can't conversationally control the group, I decline the invitation. I think ahead and play out hypothetical conversations so I'm prepared. I lie awake at night rehearsing a bothersome interaction if it didn't go well. I can't move on.

Wonder, though, makes us peer through the door. The Mass was the key to my rediscovery of wonder. Such a simple action, ritual and formal, and yet it reveals new wonder every day. It became the key that unlocked the wonder of everyday life. It's easy to wonder at the launching of a spaceship, a major disaster, a world-historic event, but the Mass showed me to marvel at the taste of a cold cup of water, the sweetness of honey, and my firstborn daughter lying warm against my cheek. Pulled out of my ingratitude and egotistical drive to magnify so-called great events of much importance, I now see that literally everything is amazing.

The liturgy is the antidote to self-consciousness. It heals the egotistical desire to control and heals our wounded aversion to vulnerability. We can trust Jesus. Being present at the Mass, His Holy Sacrifice, removes my personality from the equation and subsumes me into His priesthood. He prays in us. He speaks from the altar. Not me. Pride is left at the door. That's enormously freeing.

Beauty is nothing if it isn't sacrifice. Because sacrifice is love, all beauty communicates love. There's the love of the artist for the thing made and also an invitation to meet the artist in that love, to share the sacrifice by being drawn into the transcendent. The Sacrifice of the Mass broke my self-consciousness by focusing attention on Christ. His love has nothing to do with my ability to contribute, earn, or even comprehend. Christ does the work, I humbly accept.

Every facet of the Mass speaks to its nature as sacrifice — the prayers, focus, unity, sense of presence at the foot of the Cross, silence, reverence. It's the same act, authored by Christ, speaking the word *love* over and over. Kneeling in the pew, wearing a suit and bowtie while my children climbed all over me, in those early days of my Catholicism I was released. I couldn't understand how, and didn't explicitly know yet I'd been led through the door to freedom. But I was free.

It was a long road. When I first realized I couldn't be Pentecostal anymore and tried out the Episcopalians at Church of the Holy Spirit, I didn't feel threatened the way I did in a Catholic church. If you've never been to an Episcopalian church, it's similar in many ways to a Catholic parish, but it's a "safer," less messy version of Catholicism. When I entered the nave, early arrivals were quietly kneeling. Some looked at the altar, others read from red prayer books. Later, I became intimately familiar with the book, the Book of Common Prayer, but back then I had no idea how to behave. I mimicked. Other people sat quietly. I sat quietly. Unlike Pentecostal churches, it felt somehow wrong to chit-chat in the space. There was a mysterious, kindly presence lingering. There was no need to speak.

A bell rang and the opening procession began. As the altar boys processed with crucifix and candles, everyone stood, so I stood. The priest made a ritual greeting and was rewarded with a collective response. Everyone made a Sign of the Cross. I made a Sign of the Cross. Everyone sat and attended to the Scriptures. I sat and attended to the Scriptures. Everyone knelt to pray. I knelt to pray.

Some contend that ritual is stale and doesn't engage the intellect and heart. What's needed in worship is spontaneous emotional engagement. This hasn't been my experience. Ritual prayer set the Holy Spirit fluttering into the air. He had space to spread his wings, and because I wasn't trying to analyze my worship experience as I had it, I was able to notice Him. In contrast to unformed, spontaneous worship, I didn't worry when to stand or sit, puzzle out what words to use for a prayer, or seem pious in the crowd without seeming *too* pious.

To a self-conscious person, unstructured prayer is a nightmare. It envelops people like me in layers of irony, almost like we're characters in a play trying to act out a script. In Pentecostal churches, we would gather to experience God's presence through collective worship, but each approached the goal differently. Some closed their eyes. Some knelt down. Some raised both hands and swayed. Some clapped. I broke out in a cold sweat.

After Pastor Jeff wrapped up his homily in the homespun way he talked, spontaneous music might break out. Worshipers, one by one, would stand and sing. It wasn't collective or instructed; theoretically dictated by individual choice but, somehow, once that first person stood, the choice became inevitable—only a matter of time until we were all standing. I wasn't the first to rise and would've been mortified to be last. I aimed for the socially acceptable sweet spot, right in the middle, when a person might stand without cloying eagerness or grudging reluctance. Too anxious game-planning to pay attention to God, I was outside my body, watching.

Personal prayer is also difficult for the self-conscious. In my youth, I learned an endearing, conversational style of prayer. There's nothing wrong with it. Not at all. For me, however, it's stressful. When praying spontaneously, my focus isn't God but on what to say next. Prayer becomes a chore.

With Mass, the flow is reversed. God does the work. The Sacrament is authored by Christ alone. Communal prayer with form and discipline, passed down as living devotion from our ancestors, allows personal devotion to flourish, setting the mind and heart free to cooperate with the action at the altar. I join that action and grace floods from the gates of the temple. I'm still holding on for dear life, but now I'm doing so with the Church and the knowledge that Christ is sleeping in the back of the boat. Any minute now, He'll be awake.

✠ ✠ ✠

"It simply stands there in the middle of a rock-cleft valley," writes Martin Heidegger of an ancient Greek religious site. "It is the temple-work that first fits together and at the same time gathers around itself the unity of those paths and relations in which birth and death, disaster and blessing, victory and disgrace, endurance and decline acquire the shape of destiny for human being."

He pictures the temple silhouetted like a trireme against an Aegean storm, stone gleaming and graced by a hidden sun. The image reminds me of how the limestone on the gothic towers of the seminary would glow in the golden hour when I walked home in the early evening from the Sterling Library. "The Greeks," Heidegger goes on, "called this emerging and arising in itself and in all things *physis*. It clears and illuminates, also, that on which and in which man bases his dwelling. We call this ground earth."

Poetics sets us on solid ground to raise a sacred house. The presence of the sacred in our midst is like a brilliant spear cast into the storm, thrust into the side of Christ. From His wounded side we are born. Heidegger uses the example of a pagan temple. I'm gesturing wildly, in comically caricatured gestures like a toddler, directly to the Mass.

We carry God's sacred, world-building beauty with us, wherever we go, a truth that is elegantly illuminated with the final words of the priest—*Ite, Missa est*. Go, the Mass is ended. It's over, but it's really not, because we carry the mission, the *missa*, with us. The redemptive work is accomplished in the liturgy, but it's only the beginning. Inevitably, the liturgy will redeem all of creation until everything is the Church. We're the sparks that start the fire.

No need to brag about it, though, or be self-conscious. Christ is in the temple. He is the poet of the temple. Our vocation is humble. Hold open the door with Him. We're porters.

Sometime in my first semester at Yale, I realized that I could literally sit in on any class I wanted. Harold Bloom was in the English department, an old man nearing the end of his career, in his estimation a dinosaur. He wasn't without his faults, but studying under his direction was a chance I couldn't pass up. I audited his class *The Agon of American Poetry*, after which I returned for several subsequent poetry seminars.

No matter the title of a class Bloom offered, the content was the same. He had a classroom with two large wooden tables in the center. On all four wainscoted walls were chalkboards upon which he wrote out the titles of perhaps a hundred poems—works by Walt Whitman and Hart Crane. He intended to discuss these poems in a single class period. Instead, he digressed so far, and his interpretations were so detailed, that we were lucky to read even a single poem.

Bloom talked for hours. He poured out random, sometimes incoherent, sometimes dead wrong but often staggeringly brilliant thoughts about poetry. He connected a random word in one poem to another with zero context. We listened for hours, we student-sardines packed into that room sitting two deep around the table, over-achieving ivy-leaguers desperately taking notes so we would never, ever forget his thoughts. They came from some cavernous place buried within him, rattling forth perhaps never to be heard again once they were uttered. I don't think even he knew what he was going to say next.

He presided, elderly, overweight, morally ambiguous. We soaked it in, chasing flights of fancy from our professor as far afield as he was inclined to drift. I was surrounded by brilliant, motivated academics, people whose clothes smelled of library book mold. I read the poems. Nodded my head. Listened. Knowing all the while that, compared to these people, I was a fraud.

Ego is loss of hope, a terminal spiritual disease. It stopped me dead in my tracks the more I allowed it grow.

Josef Pieper says hope reaches with a restless but confident heart toward the future. It's linked to the virtues of magnanimity and humility.

Magnanimity is the mindset toward greatness. It climbs the higher mountain and runs the longer distance. Liturgically, magnanimity strives for the best — sacred music sung by a well-trained schola, the most beautiful vestments, a gorgeous architectural space, serious altar boys who work with military precision. Magnanimity also includes assistance from the faithful dressed in their Sunday best, unafraid to enter sacred time, to set aside practical concerns and breathe from a different atmosphere. Nothing but the best for Christ. Nothing but the best from His Bride.

Humility, as Pieper defines it, "rests on an interior decision of the will." Humility is a choice. Every day. It arises from inner disposition. Lip service isn't enough. Over decades of attending Mass, it's become painfully clear that, if I would offer true worship, my inner self must first be converted. Ego has to go. Humility fixes our eyes solely on our Lord. The human community, as wonderful as it might be, isn't why we get up early on Sunday morning. Staring at each other is a drag. Listening to me ramble from the ambo is hit-or-miss. The reason for our communal gathering is to turn and face Jesus together.

As I refine the art of celebrating Mass, more and more my personality is left aside. Humility dictates that I pray clearly but gently, not dramatically, not interjecting my commentary or personality quirks. Humility means obedience to the Church, praying reverently, using some Latin as the Church asks, some chant, and embodying the rubrics that govern the movement of a priest at the altar. The *ars celebrandi* is the art of getting out of the way so God can love His people.

All the poetics of the Mass insist that God is greater and I am lesser.

The Mass removes doubt that all grace falls from His hand. In a strange way, I became more dissatisfied as pretensions fell away, a holy dissatisfaction. I was ejected from the false, pale sanctuary I'd built with ego and thrown into a cosmos of bright colors and solid shapes, a landscape hallowed by the sacred. Suddenly, here was true insight into who I am and how far I must travel. Taking up that challenge is a heroic, humbling task, but that's what it means to hope.

✠ ✠ ✠

Lots of monastery doorkeepers have become saints. There's something about the vocation of welcoming strangers that encourages sanctity.

St. Benedict instructed his porters (wise elderly women, every one of them), "As soon as anyone knocks or a poor person hails her, let her answer 'Thanks be to God' or 'A blessing!' Then let her attend to them promptly, with all the meekness inspired by the fear of God and with the warmth of charity."

If physically holding open a door develops love, what inner change might occur in us if we hold open the door to Heaven by living poetically?

✠ ✠ ✠

Ego insists on originality. Doing it *my* way. Wendell Berry describes the disastrous results: "Works of pride, by self-called creators, with their premium on originality, reduce the Creation to novelty—the faint surprises of minds incapable of wonder." In other words, pride falls flat.

Liturgical novelty is disastrous because it's a sign of discontented pride. Constantly updated music, tinkering with texts, strange vestments, dramatic extras, clearing away the old to make room for the new—it's all ego. For me as the priest, or the musicians, or anyone else to take center-stage disconnects creativity from what came before. It takes us out of the story the Church has been writing for generations.

Originality is loneliness, cutting us off from the communion of saints and, in so doing, cutting us off from the beauty we're incapable of creating in isolation. Creativity requires diversity. It's a large circle within which, as Berry says, we listen to, "a music so subtle and vast that no ear hears it except in fragments."

The further I humble my ego to pray with our ancestors, the more creative power the Mass exerts both over me personally and the parish I pastor. Wonder of wonders.

✠ ✠ ✠

The first Corpus Christi festivities I ever attended were at the Cathedral Basilica in St. Louis. I was skeptical of Adoration of the Blessed Sacrament. My lingering Anglican prejudice held that the Sacrament was for eating, not for display. I was Catholic, though, and wanted to throw myself entirely into it.

The Cathedral is an imposing gray-bricked, semi-Byzantine pile stacked between two sturdy towers and crowned with an elegant dome built at the height of prosperity in the decades around the 1904 World's Fair, which was hosted down the street in the largest urban park in the United States, Forest Park.

The Corpus Christi procession is massive, shutting down Lindell Boulevard. Residents of the high-rises across the street appear on balconies to gawk as Catholics pour out the church doors while chanting eucharistic hymns. Lines of altar boys lead the way. Knights of Columbus in dress uniform, plumage waving in the breeze, keep order. Children dart between groups of mothers. Fathers in suits and ties hold young children in their arms. Habited nuns and seminarians walk side-by-side with the homeless. Random cyclists and pedestrians pause out of respect.

Cardinal Raymond Burke was the homilist. What he said humbled me. He quoted from Exodus,

> Now the house of Israel called its name manna; it was like coriander seed, white, and the taste of it was like wafers made with honey. And Moses said, "This is what the Lord has commanded: 'Let an omer of it be kept throughout your generations, that they may see the bread with which I fed you in the wilderness, when I brought you out of the land of Egypt.'" (Exod. 16:31–32, RSVCE)

I, with a graduate degree in theology, who read classical Greek and quoted Aristotle, who took such pride in intellectual rigor, had never noticed this Scripture. It seems that Adoration of the Blessed Sacrament is scriptural and the Church is better at interpreting her own book than I am.

In that instant, I knew I hadn't made a mistake in converting. I gladly took a place in the crowd and followed our Lord through the streets of St. Louis, heading west down Lindell toward the dying sun.

✠ ✠ ✠

Jacques Maritain says that poetic knowledge is "quite different from mystical experience." It's a form of knowledge that belongs to everyone. We needn't possess grand spiritual gifts of mystical insight. All we need to do is give ourselves to it.

What I'm keen for you to understand is that the Mass unlocks the poetry of daily life. Its beauty isn't superfluous. It will save you. As insightful as mystical and intellectual knowledge, the poetic knowledge holds open the door to sainthood. We live the humble lives we have been given, live them poetically, to the fullest. Because everything about you is important. Everything you love, God loves.

Poetry is *making*. Knowledge made incarnate, overflowing with spiritual abundance, so much so that we can hardly wrap our arms around it. In the Basilica that day on Corpus Christi, my pretensions dropped. I was simultaneously happy and sad—it's a misconception that we cannot be both at once—by the feeling of having drunk deeply of clear cool water while leaning over the precipice of a bottomless pool. This superabundance unleashes itself in creative beauty. It can do no less.

"Let anyone who has an ear listen to what the Spirit is saying to the churches," says the Lord. "To everyone who conquers I will give some of the hidden manna" (Rev. 2:17).

✠ ✠ ✠

As a writer, I often wonder if my words have value. I want to be read. I like positive feedback. Bonus points if you tell me I'm a tortured genius.

It's clear that my egotistical desire for an audience is misguided. Jacques Maritain points out that the value of art isn't located where we think:

> The activity of art refers essentially to the need to speak and to achieve manifestation in a work-to-be-made out of a spiritual super-abundance, even though (what would, moreover, be a cruel anomaly) there may be nobody to see this work or to hear it.

A poet writes for beauty. Ideally, the creative act is met with a positive response, but if it doesn't, it's still valuable. The beauty has been made. It exists. And, if anything, I'm less searching for an audience than extending an olive branch of friendship.

I write because I'm in love. The love of God cannot be bottled up, so I create. Maybe my work finds friends, maybe it doesn't. Either way, I write.

I will never cease offering the Mass, either. Even if no one is in church—again, less as an audience and more as friends participating in the sacrifice—I'll celebrate the Mass for sheer love, an act of sacrificial beauty in the midst of a world ugly with sin. My hope is that numerous faithful join and we create an even greater artifact of beauty, but, even if they don't, the Mass is infinitely valuable. The world is a better place for its having been offered.

In a stunning turn of events, God consents to speak. His purpose isn't, perhaps, what we think. The Mass isn't a practical communication of abstract intellectual content. It's the unfolding of friendship, through poetry, through grace, inside of us. We are not audience. We are friends. The poem imposes the image of Christ, the Word, upon us. We put on His likeness and become walking expressions of undying love, a love so strong it cannot be silent even if no one listens.

The poetics of the Mass require that we place our whole selves in God's hands, trusting the Church even when we don't understand what a symbol means or what possible justification there could be for Corpus Christi processions. We humble ourselves for the poem. We humble ourselves because that's what friendship does.

Like disappearing into the trees, disappear into the image of Christ.

☩ ☩ ☩

When Robinson Crusoe is shipwrecked, he inventories the items that have been salvaged from the sea. The list is a poetry of limits.

There are tools and provisions he no longer possesses. They aren't listed. In the same way, imagination only works with what we know.

Hope is concrete. We reach out to possibilities and the imagination hints at what lies beyond the horizon, but there's always an inventory, a humbling admission of boundaries. My hope is to be a human being fully alive, not God.

Between limitation and imagination is self-knowledge, a description of what I am and what I am not. Self-knowledge isn't artificially self-debasing any more than it's egotistical. It's accurate.

Poetic space must be carved out between things lost and things hoped for. For me, these inventories create gratitude, the knowledge of how to receive from God exactly what He offers.

It would be exceedingly boorish to turn down our Lord's offer of His Body and Blood because I prefer instead a new car or promotion at work. It's common sense to accept from God what He actually gives, and to do so with astonishment.

Is the Mass an inventory, the memory of what lies under the waves? Our sins, flaws, pride, mistaken perceptions of ourselves? Acknowledgment of death and the destruction of ego? Further, is it an inventory of gratitude for what I have been given? If so, the Mass is poetry of limitation, sorting out our true stature before God. This is how we finally arrive at true self-knowledge.

☩ ☩ ☩

Consider the mystical covenant of Christ and His Bride. Wendell Berry says, "In marriage as in poetry, the given word implies the acceptance of a form that is never entirely of one's own making." Just as a marriage imposes commitments and a form of life, so too does the Mass. We voluntarily limit ourselves for the sake of the other.

The liturgy places us within a set of commitments and, if we wish to participate fully, requires humility to accept those limits by adhering to the formal nature of the relationship. This process is challenging, but I've realized I cannot live a beautiful life until I consent to speak God's nuptial language, and speak it the way it was meant to be spoken. It's not for you or me to change the Mass or sit in judgment of its form. It speaks as it speaks. Breaking the form breaks the poem.

Here's the paradox: just as marriage is a self-limiting sacrifice resulting in the creative expansion of two unified souls, so too is the Mass. The formal quality of the Mass which draws us into the boundaries of what it is — the Passion of our Lord — is an expression of hope, the hope of the martyrs, the angels, and the Church as she endures sorrow. At the altar, we await the wedding feast, preparing for Christ to make Him welcome. Abandoning form, for whatever motive — relevance, entertainment, modernity — is egotistical. It abandons the Bridegroom.

I feel a heavy responsibility to care for the formal aspects of the Mass. I strive to celebrate as a custodian. I want to pass it on, just as I learned it, to the next generation. It's my gift to them.

The form is delicate, shattering in our hands if we aren't careful. Once lost, it's extremely difficult to recover. All the power of Hell fights it.

I suppose what I find most difficult in submitting to the form of the Mass is precisely what makes it so special. I must cede control. I cannot be the author. My commitment to the nuptial bond must be absolute, my love unconditional. The generosity of soul required is a constant battle against ego. I must give myself wholly to God — thoughts, desires, hopes, opinions — or the poem will become a lifeless thing in my grasping hands.

There are certainly times when the burden of the Mass, the word it speaks, seems wrongly given. Why can't it be less mysterious and archaic? But God reminds me, time and again, that this is the

Mass that speaks us into existence, creates saints, and is redeeming the cosmos. It isn't for me to doubt, introduce my own forms, or seek the false freedom of formlessness. At best, I would introduce confusion. At worst, dissolve the marriage.

Traditional forms of the Mass, practiced gently and lovingly, should not be abandoned. They're freeing, summoning unknown possibility, invoking hope and beauty. As Berry says, "Form, strictly kept, enforces freedom."

When I read poetry, it creates difficulties. Verses, allusions, metaphors I can't figure. I remember venturing an interpretation of a poem once in Harold Bloom's class. He looked at me with pity. That's how wrong I was. I would have done far better to have spent more time with the poem and practiced meekness before the mystery. The Mass, too, halts us before its majesty. In our impatient pride, we insist on an interpretation we aren't qualified to apply, and it comes to pieces in our fingers. Refusal of limitation leads to destruction of our precious heritage. I wonder if God is shaking His head.

The discomfort of the mystery is precisely why it exists. It's the true occasion of the poem. Only when we bow before it do we grow. The boundaries imposed, the need to fit ourselves to the Mass instead of demanding that it fit to us, turns us from false pretension.

In processing my reception in the Church, it's clear that the Mass deflected me back onto God's path. It has left me continually searching out that path. Before, I was certain of everything. Now, I hold my ideas cautiously, but whereas the door had been tightly closed, it's now wide open.

"The keeping of the form instructs us," writes Berry. "The world, the truth, is more abounding, more delightful, more demanding than we thought. What appeared for a time perhaps to be mere dutifulness, that dried skull, suddenly breaks open in sweetness—and we are not where we thought we were, nowhere that we could have expected to be." This has been my experience. There's power in poetic form, a precious treasure. Only by staying and attending can we learn something of the unity, the majesty, the splendor of God. He makes Himself intelligible, but only if we join in His formal communication do we join our hearts to His. As Berry puts it, "Joining the form, we join all that the form has joined."

✠ ✠ ✠

We carry interpretive baggage into conversations, perceptions, and relationships. My ego colors my worldview to the extent that I literally think every conversation, every headline news story, every decision made in a far-off distant land by some random political leader, is about me. I wonder why they're all out to get me. Then, later, I wonder how all my beliefs became so inaccurate.

As David Foster Wallace told a bunch of kids at a graduation, "A huge percentage of the stuff that I tend to be automatically certain of is, it turns out, totally wrong and deluded.... Here is just one example of the total wrongness of something I tend to be automatically sure of: everything in my own immediate experience supports my deep belief that I am the absolute center of the universe; the realest, most vivid and important person in existence. We rarely think about this sort of natural, basic self-centeredness because it's so socially repulsive. But it's pretty much the same for all of us."

I could have used that advice as a child, a warning to not let my ego become so urgent, so all-powerful in shaping my perspective. Really, in the end, all I've achieved through ego is isolation.

A poem dissolves egotistical, isolated worldviews into a much larger, shared experience. The Mass infuses the perspective of Christ, who is love, hope, and faith. His Word is already packed with meaning that I can no more alter than the setting of the sun tonight. That Word has already been in conversation with the Church for thousands of years.

As a writer, I search out new words, occasionally putting one to use, but the goal is creating a work to contribute to an ongoing conversation. Otherwise, I speak only to myself. Humility is required to work within a community, accepting tradition, other writers, and dictionary definitions. Stepping into something bigger than me, I'm a student, not a master.

Ego is a defense mechanism for self-consciousness, low self-esteem, anxiety, loneliness, lack of meaning. I put on my armor, puff my feathers, pretend I'm stronger and tougher than I am. It's an illusion that I've painstakingly been peeling away to become more honest and vulnerable. I've become less self-conscious, hopefully more kind and patient. Most of all, the destruction of ego through the Mass has allowed me to accept myself, a flawed guy who God nevertheless loves.

The first homily I ever preached was laughable. It was stuttered from a bundle of nerves. The first Mass I sang squeaked out from vocal cords so tight they could've popped like a balloon. I still barely know how to be a father, a husband, or a priest. My hair is graying. The parishioners have started a drinking game based on how many obscure poets I mention each week. They all think I'm slightly daft.

I love it all, because I know God loves it all. We don't have to be perfect before He loves us. We simply need to kneel before His altar with open hearts and allow Him to continue writing the poem.

Joni Eareckson Tada describes herself as *poiema* in her book *A Place of Healing*, writing that God

> is the Master Artist or Sculptor, and He is the One Who chooses the tools He will use to perfect His workmanship. What of suffering, then? What of illness? What of disability? Am I to tell Him which tools He can use and which tools He can't use in the lifelong task of perfecting me and molding

me into the beautiful image of Jesus? Do I really know better than Him, so that I can state without equivocation that it's always His will to heal me of every physical affliction?

If I am His poem, do I have the right to say, "No, Lord. You need to trim line number two and brighten up lines three and five. They're just a little bit dark."

Do I, the poem, the thing being written, know more than the poet?

When I approached the archbishop in St. Louis about becoming Catholic and being ordained to the priesthood, he recommended spiritual direction. I had no clue what spiritual direction was, so at our first session I narrated my life story. I talked about Pentecostalism, marrying young, becoming Episcopalian, going to seminary, becoming Anglican, planting churches in Cape Cod, and realizing I needed to be Catholic. To me, it seemed a natural progression. To my spiritual director, it sounded like a lot of movement very quickly. To me, it was a decade, a long time. To him, it was a decade, a short time to make two separate religious conversions. Adding to the changes, I was proposing to quit my job, sell my house, and move my family across the country to St. Louis. It made perfect sense—at least until my new spiritual director began asking questions. Why now? Why the priesthood? What if Catholicism becomes tiresome? Where is all this heading? It wasn't that I didn't have answers so much as it hadn't even occurred to me to ask those questions.

Pride and self-confidence are flip sides of the same personality trait. I act swiftly when I make a decision, but becoming Catholic isn't like switching Protestant denominations, and ordination to priesthood is irrevocable. I saw why my spiritual director was cautious and wanted me to slow down and widen my perspective.

The answers, when they came, arrived with the Lord in the Mass. My vocation and destiny couldn't come from within, no matter how self-confident I was. Only God could supply answers. If I wanted to hear them, I needed to humble myself and listen.

For so many years I'd felt abandoned. The spiritual leaders I'd admired at Oral Roberts were, one by one, exposed as bad shepherds, emotionally abusive men who took advantage of their flock. In the Episcopal church, the scenario repeated itself and I felt abandoned as dogma after dogma of the faith was thrown away by their pastors. I knew families who, with great sadness, left the churches their grandparents had built. Some lost their faith entirely over the betrayal they experienced. I never lost my faith, but I did wrap it tightly into my ego. In order to spiritually survive, I was convinced I had to be very strong and decisive and take care of myself.

The Mass resisted my survival techniques, unfolding with maddening subtlety, the priesthood parting like the Red Sea to reveal the presence of God Himself in the Blessed Sacrament. This, I couldn't dominate. My ego crashed against the Eucharist and lost. As the Psalmist admits, "You overwhelm me with all your waves" (Ps. 88:7). I was plunged into an emotional journey that's hard to describe because it opened up a resonance that sensitized me to the work of the Holy Spirit. It cracked my ego and showed I didn't have to hold on so tightly. I could let go and trust.

Christ is a true shepherd who authors within us only beauty. Perhaps the unexplainable, and difficult to accept, change within me was caused by meeting, for the first time, a spiritual Father who wouldn't abandon me. It wasn't a question any longer of locating a pastor who was good and holy enough to never disappoint. Suddenly, my spiritual health dug down to the very bedrock, to Christ Himself. Every day, without fail, He is there.

I didn't shed my ego right away. After all, I'd been indulging in arrogance for decades, but from that moment, the vice lost its toehold. To this day, I'm still discerning what it means to stand in the presence of God during the Mass, to place my heart in His hands.

In an experience that lovers of poetry will find familiar, this divine poem has possessed me entirely and created new realities. Beyond sentiment, damaged emotions, and personal failings, there it is, the pearl of great price.

The word *stanza* means "room," a space in which we dwell, brought into this heavenly mansion by beauty. At the threshold, I pause. There, at the bottom step of the altar, I recite the preparatory prayers. I want to madly rush up, but it's an act of humility, this pause before ascending, an acknowledgment that I'm a flawed, limited man. So I linger a moment and beg God's mercy. Then, assured by the ritual poetry of the Mass, I step into the embrace of my High Priest.

In the curve of the apse, the air gains voice and evens out the untrained waver in my song. It's the thin singing of a priest which contrasts so unadvantageously with the voices in the schola. A lesson in vulnerability. The path is a humble one, trusting that my meager gift will be met with encouragement and, indeed, in the very act of giving and receiving, will be transformed into something beautiful.

As a child, at bedtime I would lie under the covers in my darkened room. The only light came from the open door to the hall. My father would always look in on me before passing on to his bedroom, his figure silhouetted against the light. My father standing in the door. I fell asleep knowing I was safe.

EIGHT

All Dreams Are Vexing

FOR A LONG time, I found the Mass strange, undeniably beautiful but punctuated by stretches of boredom. I struggled to maintain focus. The action around the altar struck me as artificial and contrived. It felt long. Toddlers shuffled in the pews. The air conditioning unit kicked on, barely stirring the dense air. Meanwhile, the priest was bent low over the altar, whispering. Later, I realized my difficulty was because of disordered desire. I was swimming in the shallows of cheap sentiment, emotional comfort, and easy consolations. My soul wasn't shaped toward contemplation and sacrifice, wasn't yet ready to conform to the will of God and love what He loves. Beyond that insight, though, lies a startling truth. God's beauty is just plain difficult.

The Mass rests on our shoulders like a strange garment. Life does the same.

Anticipating his death, W. S. Merwin writes,

Then I will no longer
Find myself in life as in a strange garment
Surprised at the earth
And the love of one woman

And the shamelessness of men
As today writing after three days of rain
Hearing the wren sing and the falling cease
And bowing not knowing to what.

I've had similar experiences of stunned wonder, arriving from some unheralded origin and swiftly disappearing, leaving me short of breath. Standing in the grass in the countryside, surrounded by the haunted cries of weaning calves for their mothers; carrying my tired daughter on my back along a forest trail in the midst of a surprise rain shower, her chubby toddler legs dangling down and swinging with every step, her fingers digging into my ribs; eating oysters bedded in saltwater while on the deck of a Cape Cod fish house overlooking Wellfleet Bay, where the water retreats with the moon to expose miles of ocean floor, pooled and glassy in the late summer sun. It happens regularly during the Mass.

Christ has authored a strange language. Catholics, perhaps, are unaware of how odd they seem to outsiders. John Adams, for instance, attended a Mass in Philadelphia in 1774 and described it to his wife Abigail:

The poor wretches fingering their beads, chanting Latin, not a word of which they understood, their Pater Nosters and Ave Marias. Their holy water — their crossing themselves perpetually — their bowing to the name of Jesus wherever they hear it — their bowings, and kneelings, and genuflections before the altar. The dress of the priest was rich with lace — his pulpit was velvet and gold. The altar piece was very rich — little images and crucifixes about — wax candles lighted up. But how shall I describe the picture of our Saviour in a frame of marble over the altar, at full length, upon the cross in the agonies, and the blood dropping and streaming from his wounds.

He seems simultaneously revolted and attracted, a feeling I once shared. The Mass is comfort and exile, possessing deep spiritual solace but always a foreign tongue.

This lack of constant comfort is a cardinal sin to modern man. We hate the idea that we cannot control every element of existence. It's a shame, because endless comfort introduces mediocrity. If we cannot grasp Latin, it must go. If plainchant sounds odd, get rid of it. Incense, darkness, fine vestments, any and all hints of sin and sacrifice, strike them out. Essentially, the poetry of the Mass, that which we only partially understand, must be replaced with weak comfort, relevance, easily digestible communication. In doing so, transcendence is flattened. The Mass is empty. Everything that horrified John Adams disappears and we become respectable.

The thing is, I don't want to be respectable. I want to be a saint. I want to feel poetry.

I don't care how frustrating, humbling, or foreign the Mass is — I don't need control. I don't need to eliminate everything I don't understand. I simply need to be loved.

Encountering God is fearful. Bigger than the night sky, beyond the limited scope of the human mind, it's the strangeness of *becoming*.

Merwin notices it, that struggle of pushing forward into the unknown, how each year the anniversary of his future death spins around and he lives through it, not knowing the date. How very strange, to be aware of this, each moment a tender reminder of our limits, and yet each one overflowing with eternal significance. The mystery manages, by some apocalyptic catastrophe, to break through. A shiver runs down my spine; it's so beautiful. So delicate it breaks apart under the weight of becoming. It's all too much.

Maybe this is why sometimes I barely manage to whisper through the prayers. The strange garment covers us, descending like a coat of many colors onto our bent shoulders.

What are we becoming?

It's delicate but inevitable, this divine love which goes out in weakness and returns as conqueror of sin and death.

We make a grave mistake to minimize this strangeness. To do so destroys the poetic and closes the gap between who we are and who God is. It's a gap that we aren't qualified to close. Yes, God is relatable and personal. He loves us intimately, but He's still God and we His creatures. In that distinction is birthed the miracle of poetry. The strangeness is how we feel beauty.

The Mass clothes us in Christ, the heavenly garment, the day of our death cycling around again and again, containing future promise. Owen Barfield says that poetry is impossible without this movement. In the Mass, the movement is the lifting up of our heart to God, the descent of the Spirit on the gifts, the offering up of the sacrifice by Christ our High Priest, and the return of love signifying acceptance of that sacrifice. These movements are strange to us because they take place in the realm of grace. They aren't within our natural abilities, but without them the Mass is stillborn. Our hearts are stilled.

God is progressively incarnating grace into our world, weaving a coat against winter's freeze, the bright wing of the Holy Spirit overshadowing the womb, fire-fangled, startling in the thaw as He perches ever so lightly because, soon enough, He must fly. Perhaps we will rise with Him to see, even if briefly, further than we've ever seen before, out over frost-hardened field to the white-hot sun that brightens it to diamond.

The father said to his servants, "Quickly, bring out a robe—the best one—and put it on him" (Luke 15:22).

☩ ☩ ☩

Why doesn't poetry say exactly what it means? Why do we have to sit with it, examine it, discuss it?

The poem *does* say exactly what the poet wants to say. That's the point. It's simply that we're unprepared. The meaning is shrouded because the Mass expresses a living faith that dwells beyond words. Through symbolic language it creates unity of concrete and abstract, physical and metaphysical, truth and beauty. It expresses the fullness of reality. This is why, when asked about the meanings of certain liturgical actions, all I can do is shrug.

It cannot be intellectualized. We are embodied creatures, a marriage of spirit and body. So is the incarnated Christ, and it is He who words the Mass.

Catholics think like poets, both in our churches and our lives. A poet possesses a sacramental outlook, attentive to higher meanings within particulars. Christ is not separate from the physical world. He inhabits it. He makes it beautiful.

Faith isn't content with the mere collection of facts. The Mass isn't successful because of the information contained in the homily or because the priest delivers explanatory asides. It isn't successful only if we perfectly comprehend it. Comprehension is the first step, because of course we must know the One we love, but His depths are endless. Above all else, the Mass invites us into a relationship. Like a husband and wife who, through their shared life together, know each other more intimately every day even until death do them part, so too do we know God.

✠ ✠ ✠

Friends of mine have mentioned experiences similar to mine of attraction and repulsion at the Mass. They acknowledge its beauty but comment that, long term, it isn't for them. They prefer other forms of prayer or even Masses that have been divested of mystery in the name of relevance. These are more easily digestible. This is sad because easy worship is mediocre prayer.

For me, the challenge of participating didn't reveal flaws in the Mass but, rather, a fault line within myself. I was the one who needed to change. The poem was difficult and frustrating. It handed me a cross and asked me to carry it next to Christ in the dark night. Exactly what I needed. What we all need. To this very day, I go up to the altar mumbling Psalm 42, "Why do I go sorrowful?" (Ps. 42:2, DRA).

Without the Mass we are nothing. The future of the Church depends on protecting it. Without its poetry, beauty, and mystery we're far from the Cross, far from the heart of Christ. This negatively affects our spiritual lives but also the entire scope of our lives.

Don't be content to wrap a garment of leaves around yourself as you march out of Eden. If you find the Mass difficult, don't give up or change it. Instead, surrender. Ask God to open your heart to His divine communication. Make yourself ready to hear. Trust the Church. This is how Christians have prayed for thousands of years. The Mass has nurtured saints.

In the early days of my priesthood, I practiced and refined my sacramental role. As I did so, Christ readjusted my identity. He taught me to rest in His presence. My passions, which had been desperate for entertainment, something to consume or do, were retrained. I internalized the outward form of the Mass and the inward meaning unfolded.

In the presence of sacred beauty, worldly cares recede. Hunger recedes, thirst remains unquenched, and time becomes recollected into poetic memory that bespeaks creation itself. A prayerful, contemplative, humble interior posture is difficult to achieve. From the outside, many who are actively and fully participating will seem to be doing nothing.

The Mass is both feast and fast because the Bridegroom isn't yet fully present. There's a sense of loss and unrequited sadness as He slips away and we shuffle out the church doors.

The greatest art requires the greatest sacrifice, so of course we hesitate. The Mass is the greatest of all art. It rearranges our lives most thoroughly and confronts us with chaste, unyielding beauty. To participate in it, we must first be remade. The poetics are unsparing.

Personally, I'm honored to slip on my strange garment and intercede at the altar. My heart trembles at the difficulty of what God asks of us, contrasted by the ease with which He forgives, accepts, and loves us.

I'm a leaf, shaken from a tree and falling.

☩ ☩ ☩

Henri Bergson was fond of saying, "I have suffered from this friend enough to know him." This is how I feel about the Mass, which has caused me a fair bit of suffering. In order to become Catholic, I had to sell our family home, move my wife and children into temporary housing in a new city, quit my job and accept a lower-paying job, leave dear friends behind, introduce tension into my wider family over the conversion, and throw my entire future into question.

It's funny—reading that list makes it seem a lot more difficult than I remember. I do remember stress and sadness over the changes, but it never felt like real suffering, not like the great martyrs. And to be honest, it really wasn't that difficult, but I also don't want to deny that these were genuine obstacles. In traversing them I came to live the Mass in a peculiar way.

Throughout our lives, we're in motion whether we like it or not. The difficulty is choosing the path—stumble downstream, or fight like crazy to resist the current—it's ours to decide. The difficulty brings beauty to fruition. Suffering is a love letter.

I'm not quite sure what I would, or would not, endure in order to participate in the Mass. I'd like to think I'd trade the whole world. I'd like to think that, if I had to, I'd happily offer Mass in a prison cell. Who knows? At the very least, I make my best offering, pour out a vessel of my most precious perfume. The perfume jar, of course, only gives up its treasure once it's broken.

✠ ✠ ✠

Poetry is obscure. Its aim is not easy comprehension but, rather, to impart grace. Our first instinct is to rewrite or clean it up, thinking it will benefit from clarification. This urge is ever-present with the Mass. I'm going to say this as gently as possible—we cannot tinker with the poem and expect it to live. If Christ is to throw off the grave-clothes, He must do so buried deeply in the tomb, in His own time, and only by way of the Passion. All the important work of the Mass is done in the darkness that begins at the Cross and doesn't end until the stone is rolled from the grave.

This has been my practical experience in my life as well. All that is precious—my faith, marriage, children, time spent with good friends, the almost delirious joy of waking up each morning—has crystalized out of an incomprehensible depth of meaning, a binding oath that holds me in thrall and from which I wouldn't escape even if I could. Buried with God in baptismal water, covered in His Blood, stripped bare at the Cross, our days are marked by trial, by the friction between life and death. So where is Christ in all this? The Mass provides the answer. He is buried with us. He rises with us. As the Introit for pastors rejoices, "In the midst of the church he opened his mouth.... He clothed him with a robe of glory."[3]

In *Gravity and Grace*, Simone Weil claims the absence of mercy here below is actually a sign that God exists. I don't agree that mercy is absent, but her point is valid that life isn't easy. At times,

---

[3] This is a paraphrase of Sirach 15:5 from the Common of Doctors of the Church in the old missal.

it's downright nasty. For some far more so than others, which is, of course, unfair. Life brings suffering, no matter how we wriggle and try to escape. However, this seeming lack of mercy juxtaposed with beauty is revelatory. Annie Dillard comments, "Life's cruelty joins the world's beauty and our sense of God's presence to demonstrate exactly who we're dealing with, if dealing we are: God immanent and transcendent ... God beside us and wholly alien."

The Mass is a warm, familiar homecoming; it is also deeply unsettling. God is far away, enthroned in majesty; God is with us, bending low to hear the whispered romances of His Bride.

As Wallace Stevens writes, "It was her voice that made / the sky acutest at its vanishing."

✠ ✠ ✠

If I were to define bad art, it would be a made thing that forces prepackaged emotions onto us. For instance, a birthday card with a sappy, sentimental phrase printed inside. A nice thought, and certainly appreciated, but not good art. It attempts to prompt an appropriate reaction, but in fact a greeting card has nothing to do with love or gratitude or sorrow. It claims the power of real emotion, but emotions are hard-won. I accept premade cards with gratitude but after a few weeks dispose of them. The handmade drawings my children present to me I keep forever.

The Mass cannot tell you how to feel. It won't — it shouldn't — emotionally manipulate you. If you're sad, you can stay sad. If grieving, linger in your grief. If happy, be confirmed in your happiness. Whatever we bring is what we leave with, because these are genuine emotions. What the Mass does, though, is provide grace to properly order those emotions and bring virtue to them. Beauty is strong enough to contain the entire range of our experience, the good and the bad, the valleys and mountains, and divine poetics cover us with the white robe of the martyrs. The good and the bad is folded into God's love.

How beautiful is that?

☩ ☩ ☩

I celebrate three Masses every Sunday. Probably too many, but it's my own fault. Three years ago, I was asked by a group of parishioners to offer an evening Traditional Latin Mass. I declined because I didn't think anybody would attend. They kept asking, politely but insistently. They told me how great it would be. They would take care of everything and all I would need to do was show up. Still, I resisted. Sunday afternoons are for watching football and drinking Pimms in the garden, not squeezing in a late lunch before heading right back to church to work more.

Around that time, though, I began digging into the history of the Mass. I became interested in celebrating it within the larger tradition of the Church. I desired to become conversant in the poetic language that the Church has been speaking for two thousand years. I wanted to know my brother priests better by praying the way they prayed.

It was a difficult educational process. I had to learn Latin and, equally importantly, needed to become comfortable reading and singing Latin out loud. My accent was, and remains, horribly anglophone. I growl out the letters in a guttural American idiom. I'm working on it and I'm getting better, I promise. I realized that in order to improve I needed steady practice. The best way to practice would be through a regular Mass. In a two-birds-one-stone epiphany, I agreed to the Sunday evening Mass using the 1962 Missal. I figured that about thirty or forty people would attend, I'd get my practice in, and that would be just fine.

The first night, about fifty people came. The week after, there were more. Then a schola formed to handle the chant. More people arrived. Large families appeared. Young adults became intrigued, fell in love with the beauty, and started registering in the parish. The average age of our parish plummeted. Originally, I had one altar server. He's now one of a dozen serious young men who are committed to their Faith. Crucifers, torchbearers, acolytes, thurifers. Men being men. Offering God their poetic best.

The new parishioners brought wine and beer and hung out in the courtyard after Mass. Children run with wild joy in the dark, playing tag among the roman columns that hold up the porch of the church. Several hundred people are now, in some way, involved in the Sunday night Mass at Epiphany of Our Lord. Their energy benefits the entire parish. Our Sunday morning Masses have also steadily improved in quality and are attracting converts. The parish children are learning to chant. Young adult groups have sprung up and are thriving. A youth group formed. A mothers' group organized. I don't know how it all happened. I just wanted to practice Latin.

Why did they come, and why do they stay?

The comment I receive most frequently is that the manner in which our parish offers the Mass is restful. It's been described as a spiritual oasis. I understand the phenomenon because I experience a strange paradox when I offer the Mass. It's the most challenging liturgy on my schedule, requiring me to concentrate on Latin and chant along with maintaining precise rubrics. Because it's last on my schedule, I arrive tired and worn out. I've preached the same homily, if you count the Saturday vigil, three times already and cannot bear hearing myself talk anymore. By Sunday evening, the sound of my own voice annoys me, and the conceit that a poor soul would hear me and think my words anything more than insipid posturing is mildly amusing. The parishioners don't know what they're in for. I already know one of my practical examples fell flat. It's been cut from the text. Any passion I had for the theme has long since drained away and I can only throw my poor efforts at the feet of God and hope He can somehow enliven them. My singing voice wavers, victimized by hours of talking and cup after cup of espresso.

This is when plain old stubbornness comes to the rescue. I made the commitment to offer this Mass and will keep it. I down another cup of coffee, put on my surplice to go hear confessions, and then go to greet the gathered servers in the sacristy.

This is my attitude before Mass. After, it's different. I'm calm and relaxed. I look forward to talking with parishioners in the courtyard. We send the kids down the block for snow cones and mingle. The Mass, you see, has not made me tired. It has given me life.

I've thought a lot about this—why the more elaborately beautiful a Mass is, the more spiritually nourishing it becomes. It's as if the difficulty breaks open a hidden moment with God. We sit with Him at the foot of the Cross, succor Him, and so hold Him until it is revealed that, all along, He was the one strong enough to hold us. The chant, so pure and limpid, is a lullaby sung from Mary to her child, from a people to their Crucified Savior. It surrounds us and, just for the precious hour we're gathered, the sound of traffic on the road outside muffles, and the white noise that followed us in, the buzzing in our ears, quiets. Weariness falls away like a stone dropped from the hand and our souls enter into God's rest, not His eternal rest, not quite yet, but a foretaste.

As the Carthusians say, "Stat crux dum volvitur orbis." The world turns and the Cross remains.

As a father of six children and spiritual father to many more, I've learned how a father loses a piece of himself to his children. Their interests become mine, their lives take priority, and their flourishing is more important than all else. In that sacrificial exchange, as any parent can tell you, I didn't lose myself. I found myself. My identity, through the miracle of love, is enriched. From the first moment I held my firstborn in my arms I knew I was a new man and that, with my daughter's birth, I had been born again. With each child this has happened again. In the Mass, I have never ceased being born again.

This is the secret to why the Mass, even as it opens a wound in our side and we lose our heart to Christ, mirrors His own life-giving wound through which we are brought to birth. The more deeply I disappear and am joined to the Cross, the heavier the weight I consent to place on my shoulders, the more blessed I am. God's burden is light.

It was hard work, making this Sunday evening Mass at Epiphany happen. I've taken grief from parishioners who don't understand. They don't know why anyone would like Latin or chant or incense. They think it's all backwards, anti-modern, rigid traditionalism. I understand their hesitation. After all, learning how to offer it stripped my soul bare and I shrank back. I felt the crushing realization that, previously, I hadn't actually understood the Mass, how its poetic voice sings of another world.

In the end, all I know is that difficulty unlocks beauty. Beauty cannot dissolve difficulty, but it defies the separation caused by affliction by piecing together what has been scattered. In such a way do we experience divine peace, the piece of the fractured Host and bloody chalice, a peace dearly won, not achieved, only received. It's gift, this beauteous broken Savior, God reminding us that He is our Father, and that He loses His most precious treasure for us.

✠ ✠ ✠

For so long, my life was shapeless, defined only by selfish whim. I would stay up all night. Eat whatever I wanted. Watch television all afternoon. Hibernate in my room with a book. External conditions made passing few demands on me. All I needed was to get my schoolwork done and be on time for work. Most of the day was entirely mine.

The choices I made are questionable. Wasted time. Boredom. Cheap entertainment. Doing the bare minimum to get through classwork that didn't interest me.

The Mass has broken me of this bad habit of throwing my time away, because, liturgically, every gesture and word counts. Poetically, each word is a hewn monument, towering and fixed, but affecting us in such a way as to impart fresh life. As Heidegger says, "Being's poem, / just begun, is man."

My parishioners tease that I'm fussy. I laugh about it. I *am* fussy. But I also like to think of myself as earnest. Surrounding myself in beauty is difficult work! I want the best coffee, good food, a real wood fire in the hearth. On a fall afternoon I wear a fine suit and leather gloves. At the altar, fine silk damask threaded with gold. The sanctuary ought to have beautiful painting. So too should a home. Art is expensive but worth it. A few times a week, when I feel ambitious, I put down the newspaper and read a poem.

Our lives are too precious to fritter away in commonplaces, so I shape my life with a form quality of beauty. By doing so, I strengthen the connection between my individual, particular existence and the primeval Goodness that universally underlies all things, bringing with it infinite value.

You and I are far too valuable to God to live sloppy, ill-considered lives defined only by comfort-seeking. We aren't scribbles on the wall. We're icons of Christ.

The Mass is far too valuable. The sound and color of it matters — meter, rhythm, shape. Here, we're talking about craft, integrity, discipline, reverence for the sacred. "The Liturgy must be regarded with at least as much respect as a profane masterpiece of this kind," writes Martin Mosebach. "Respect opens our eyes." There is no true love without reverence.

You may call it fussy. I call my attention to detail an expression of devotion. Mosebach says that, through detail, the sacred liturgy becomes "saturated with spiritual power." He goes on: "Liturgy became a rich image with a welter of tiny details, greater than the sum of its parts; thus it must be contemplated and can never be entirely understood."

The more I focus on detail, the more important those details are revealed to be. As they're respected and practiced, they're woven into a lacework of intricate beauty, a form wondrous to behold and overwhelming in perception. It's clear, in a life so lived or in a Mass so offered, that formality guards the sacred.

✠ ✠ ✠

We brought our three children into the Church with us, young enough that they only remember being Catholic. Since then, we've had three more, accidentally morphing into a shambolic, hipster, Catholic family bumping around town in our beat-up Honda minivan.

Fighting the whole time for a turn in the front seat.

Our yard is the embarrassment of the neighborhood. I gave up trying to grow grass a long time ago because our boys dig holes everywhere with toy dump trucks. I've made peace with the mess. I'm not particularly motivated to obsess over lawn care, anyways. My strategy is to refuse to water it until the grass turns brown and I don't have to mow anymore. As reparation, the yard is decorated with dirt bikes, plastic tools, and the ruins of old forts.

Inside, the house is a sight to behold. One of our blossoming little fine artists managed to scribble in permanent marker an inscrutable design all over the couch. The kitchen sink overflows with dirty dishes which teeter on the brink of avalanche. The toddler has discovered she's tall enough to reach the apple basket. She helps herself to a dozen apples per day, taking a single, careful bite out of each one before dropping it to the floor. I constantly trip on apples with tiny teeth marks in them.

In our parish, they join a veritable army of children, all of whom threaten to drag the nave into total chaos. When I'm at the altar, I hear the pitter-patter of tiny feet making mad dashes to the bathroom in the middle of prayers, attempted whispers that aren't whispers at all, and enthusiastic shouted descriptions of every action at the altar like they're narrating a nature documentary. *Mommy, he rang the bells! THE BELLS!* Last week, a little boy, desirous of starting the Mass early, rang the sacristy bell while I was still vesting and I heard the whoosh of hundreds of people obediently standing for the start of the Introit.

I wonder why I love it so much, the mayhem of childrearing. Why do reasonable, thoughtful people consent to become parents, knowing full well how overwhelming it can be? How embarrassing it is to take a child to a restaurant or endure a tantrum in the grocery store aisle? Maybe parents are all in a state of sleep-delirium from having been kicked awake all night by toddler feet. We think our lives are normal.

But, seriously, I adore it. Family is the ongoing composition of a poem that tiptoes us right to the ledge. I'm stopped cold. It's the southwest passage, an uncharted continent, perhaps the one and only discovery still worth making. Love searches it out, distills the concept of selflessness, and is prolegomena to interior immolation. Love slaughters us like lambs.

Yes, it would be wonderful to be suburban master of a lush field of green turf fronting an immaculate house, but, really, I prefer the hole to China my boys gifted me.

Parenthood destroyed illusions of a glossy, Instagrammable life. My children have formed me every bit as much as I have formed them. Together, we explore for gold and build worlds of possibility. We slip on the freshly laundered grave-clothes of our Lord. I'm living the dream, friends.

"All dreams are vexing," says Wallace Stevens.

A parish is, of course, a family. Thus the vexation, the squabbles, the feuds. When I get going about the poetic glory of the Mass, I'm not thinking of it as a performance. There's nothing professional about how we pray in our parish. The silence is punctuated by children dropping crayons to the tile. The contemplation interrupted by the occasional mobile phone dinging while a little old lady frantically digs through her purse to find it; a reader who gets confused and reads the wrong selection; a priest starting a chant on the wrong pitch. The prayers of kneeling mothers are essayed from the midst of maelstroms of children, climbing, pinching, fighting for lap space. Newcomers hide in the back. Latecomers try to slide in without being noticed. We make space for each other.

The formal nature of the Mass is that of a family, not the concert hall. The shape of devotion isn't artificial, but joins the flow of domesticity. Picture Mary, Joseph, shepherds, and bellowing animals gathered round the crib.

We aren't perfect, but beauty isn't brought to perfection by our own interior perfection. It's a quality all its own, inhering in the beauty of the *thing made*, the poem, this Mass that has emerged from generations of families at prayer, a big messy family tussling for space in the lap of our Mother, led by Christ our Brother to our Father.

A poem shows its ragged edge. It's vulnerable, flashing brilliance at times, hesitation at others, hiding, revealing. The perfection is its love. The perfection of the Mass is its love.

This is how we build culture and pass on the Faith. Like parenting, it's courageous, difficult work, the poetry of life, birth, death, children and parents, brothers and sisters, the bemused elderly, the astonishment of it all, the struggle to respond appropriately to our wonder, and love covering a multitude of sins. Wrap us in swaddling clothes, right there next to Christ, and lay us in a stone manger to be consumed.

NINE
A Second Life, Timeless and Wide

I JUST WANTED to be normal. At Oral Roberts I'd been surrounded by persuasive, outgoing, confident pastors-in-training, the type of people whose teeth sparkle when they smile, who believe God speaks directly through them prophetically. They weren't afraid to ask for donations, bluntly chastise the faithful, or predict doom for America. My classmates in seminary were the same. Future pastors as prophets, destined to remake society. Once I became a working pastor, though, I was cautious, never quite sure if I was doing or saying the right thing. At times, the vocation was disheartening. I often questioned it and struggled to love my parishioners the way they deserved to be loved. I grew jealous of pastors who had what I considered better situations than mine.

I wanted to be normal. It wasn't until much later that I realized I *was* normal. I found out later, in conversations after a minister's prayer group I was in, that everyone else was hiding their inadequacies, which were the exact same as mine. All of us pastors were secretly jealous of each other! What strange creatures we can be, so unhappy because we forget who we are and want to be something else.

Churches with historic roots, gorgeous buildings adorning town squares, and bank vaults of cash wither and fade, too tired to do anything but lay down and die. Churches fail when they forget who they are. They want to feel normal and so give away their birthright.

I saw it happen. Ensconced in Anglicanism, we were on top of the world. Privileged prospective pastors studying in the ivy league, we inherited plush parish assignments in Manhattan, Boston, and Washington, D.C. I interned at St. Paul's in Darien, Connecticut, one of the wealthiest areas on the planet. The parish was full of hedge fund managers and ex-presidential speech writers. St. Paul's is a wonderful little parish and I learned more there than I can possibly credit, but it's an exception.

The Anglican Communion is dying. The established urban parishes have professional choirs, preppy ushers in bowties, and Tiffany-designed stained glass, but the faithful are abandoning them in droves. They can't get away fast enough. *I* couldn't get away fast enough. Every day in that environment, I re-litigated my beliefs, second-guessing myself over the shifting, trendy beliefs of my church. We'd thrown away our heritage, patching the hull of our ecclesiastical ship while floating in the middle of the sea. We sank like a rock.

I can't figure exactly where the forgetting hit hardest or how it originated. If pressed for an answer, I suppose I'd point out that the splendorous truth of our faith was subsumed under the need to instrumentalize ministry. Church became a place to promote causes, spirituality a means to sociopolitical action. Dress that up with fancy theological words however you'd like, but beauty can never be an instrument. It isn't a means to an end. It isn't window dressing to the real work.

Beauty is the work. Beauty is reality. If living poetically makes me stand out from the crowd, so be it. Becoming an anonymous face isn't healthy. The quirks and wonderful little differences that set us apart, those which make us *alive*, shouldn't be erased. Being normal is nothing more than quashing diversity and sinking to the least common denominator. The soul-denying, morality-defying requirements to fit in are boring as sin, a recipe for mediocrity. To me, it felt like living in the glossy pages of a homemaking magazine. A perfect living room, spotless, trendy, fake.

Desperate to feel normal, we forget ourselves. This is what happened to me. I forgot.

Poetry is memory. This is why Dana Gioia says it "stood at the center of culture as the most powerful way of remembering, preserving, and transmitting the identity of a tribe, a culture, a nation." He then quotes Robert Frost, who called poetry "a way of remembering what it would impoverish us to forget."

Our memory of our Lord, particularly in the Mass, lifts us up into a world of transcendent good and protects us from the tyranny of fashionableness and mob mentality. We can rely on the unchanging character of God and know that His love for us and our obligations to Him extend far past the present moment. God is faithful to us and we will be faithful to Him.

Remember the saints, miracles, beauty, and answered prayer. Remember what it's like to sit in silence before the Blessed Sacrament. Remember how God has rescued you. Remember Him with gratitude and find liturgies that reverently make the space required to have a personal encounter with Christ. If your relationship with Him remains strong, it simply won't do to abandon Him. It doesn't matter what trendy, mob-induced hysteria is currently hurtling from the maelstrom. In the end, it's you and Christ.

The Gospel is a living voice. Someone is speaking to you, a poetic timbre with a quality all its own. Perhaps your father read you stories when you were young. It's the voice you remember. This voice, when it catches my attention, summons an image. I watch my son make a daring leap on the playground and am restored to an afternoon decades ago when I accomplished a similar feat. The swing gently sways and I'm sitting there again side-by-side with Amber in the park behind my house. We're teenagers. I'm about to ask her to marry me. My heart is shaking.

The image is more than a mental picture. It engages my imagination. My thoughts fly away. I even latch onto memories I never experienced. I know nothing of the castle at Brideshead or the stormy sea that destroyed the Deutschland. I've never held a Grecian urn or vacationed in Key West. But through poetic voice, I remember. The places are real. They're revelatory.

It's stunning—poetry places new reality into my consciousness across centuries of distance. I don't know how to react. I read the last page of a poem, close the book, and all I can do is hold it on my lap and sit very still.

This is how the Mass upended me. I didn't know what it was—had no clue—but as soon as I experienced it I remembered everything. I felt the wound in His side and the darkening sky at the Passion overshadowing me as I knelt on the cracked, plastic cushion of the kneeler. I knelt there, very still, reminiscing.

✠ ✠ ✠

I've always been melancholic. I lie awake in bed sweating through the sheets, insomniac, hovering over a void. I was medicated for depression as a teenager. Some days I would wake and not be able to muster even a halfhearted reason to get out of bed. I hated the sound of the alarm clock, not happy remaining in bed but unable to imagine a single activity or person that would lessen the misery. I floated in the ruined maw of emptiness.

Depression is a serious medical condition, and I don't claim the Mass will heal anyone of clinical depression. It might. But that would be a miracle, and miracles aren't formulaic. I'm confident, though, that the Mass was indispensable to my healing. It's not as though I no longer struggle with depression. I do, but it no longer breaks me.

Depression and unhappiness are not the same. I can experience depression and still be happy. Happiness is strong enough to encompass sadness, grief, spiritual desolation, material poverty, illness, disappointment, death. The Mass is healing because it reveals that happiness rests on a firmer foundation than I would have guessed. It rests on the eternally slain Lamb of God. The Host, even as it is mended back together in the hands of the priest, remains fractured down the middle, a piece gouged from its side.

Perhaps I can explain with a seemingly unrelated example: my hat. I wear a priestly hat called a *biretta*. With its black poof on top, it is, of course, whimsical. Children love it. It's also a powerful poetic symbol.

The biretta made its appearance in the depths of Church history. The word seems to be derived from *birrus*, referring to a hood. It began as more of a skull cap, but the need to take it off during Mass led to the development of three ridges at the top. Most priests don't wear it anymore, but it has a venerable place in liturgical tradition.

The biretta is put on so that it might be taken off. The sacred ministers wear it in procession to the foot of the altar, where it's removed, only to be recovered while seated and then later at the recessional. Taking it off is a physical reminder that I'm entering sacred space. The point isn't the hat itself but how, as an act of humility, it lowers my defenses and helps me pray. In this sense, it fulfills the same function as the *Confiteor* and the *Kyrie*. We throw ourselves on God's mercy. Poetry begins with humility.

My hat makes me smile. The fabric is fading to a color I can only describe as not-black, but the threadbare quality makes me love it more. It has become a visual symbol of my soul. I stand bareheaded before God. Vulnerability is my gift. I bring my arrogance, depression, flaws, entitlement, and sorrows. I bring Him quivering hands, silly concerns, stubbornness, my soul so pockmarked with sin. I'm an open book.

A spiritual space opens up in which it's acceptable to be a normal person who gets annoyed at people who leave lights on in empty rooms, has slight nerve damage in his left foot, and has a five o'clock shadow immediately after shaving. I'm empty, but not with the emptiness of depression. It's the fullness of the uncreated void, divine breath hovering, the Word speaking, and a wild parade of creatures and angels fresh and new returning His praise.

Here is where we are made. Head uncovered, I hear it in something as simple as the melismatic chant of the Introit. More than an ornament of the text, it brings meditative intensity, anticipation, this impossibly beautiful moment, as befuddling as the moment my newborn daughter was placed into my hands for the very first time.

The altar boy carries my hat away. I'm defenseless, exactly who I am, melancholic, limited, flawed, waiting. It's perfect happiness.

☩ ☩ ☩

Because of stress or plain old fecklessness, there are days I drag myself to the altar like some dead thing. A cold creature with a cold heart.

Desperate for consolation so I can wipe my failures away and stop lying awake all night obsessing, I'm horrified when God confirms there's no escaping myself. I arrive before Him exactly as I am or not at all.

Poetry reveals interior fractures. Why read a poem, then? Why allow the Mass to drag skeletons into the light? Because this is how to be a human.

I've always been keen to give God my best. I wanted to give Him my successes. He didn't want them. He wanted me. The real me.

We can't hold anything back from the sacred exchange. In thinking honestly about what I was placing on the altar to give God, I managed for the first time to make an honest interior glance. It's easy to give God our talents. Not so easy to give Him our flaws.

We're addicted to paths of least resistance. Naked honesty is terrifying, but if we cannot be ourselves with God, we'll never attain self-knowledge. For so long I was afflicted with depression but not able to fully acknowledge it, dwell with it, and give it to God. We can only give what we possess. If we don't know ourselves, we cannot give ourselves.

The suffering of self-knowledge is fundamental to happiness. The purifying flame of the Mass is unambiguous. It's not self-help. It's a mirror. It's self-fulfillment. I know this as sure as the waxen altar candles are consumed before our very eyes. God will not take the thorn from my side. He might even twist it deeper. He'll redeem it, though, and share the wound. He will baptize the suffering in love and make it beautiful.

Depression will always be with me. This side of Heaven, your flaws will more or less stick with you, too. This doesn't mean we're condemned to unhappiness. Only that we are candles meant to burn.

God makes even the wilderness beautiful. As *The Little Prince* says, "What makes the desert beautiful is that somewhere it hides a well." The Body of Christ is ever-wounded, hiding the poor suffering saints in the Mass, fire-folk etched into the fabric of the liturgy. We invoke their names and they arrive, radiant. Agnes, murdered at the age of twelve by grown men. Lucy with her eyes torn out. Lawrence making jokes while being burned to death. And then there's me. There's you. It was all I could do to focus through the Mass this morning. My thoughts swirled. I have business meetings later. The church roof needs repairs. There are people in the parish who don't like me. I stand there, damasked in silk, laced in linen. Underneath, my heart like a broken tower.

Pierre Reverdy writes, "Arise, carcass, and walk."
Can these dry bones rise?

✠ ✠ ✠

When Rainer Maria Rilke visited the sculptor Auguste Rodin in his workshop, he noticed the monkish older man had surrounded himself with his masterpieces as if they were toys. Rodin believed that art thrives in the transitional space between childhood and maturity because that's where innocence is combined with craftsmanship.

Rodin particularly loved to sculpt hands. Rilke examined the hands, hundreds of them scattered around the studio, and thought of them as an extension of the self into the wider world. Hands reach out and outline a form.

"The more deeply poetry becomes conscious of itself," writes Jacques Maritain, "the more deeply it becomes conscious also of its power to know." Ritual takes us out of time and plunges us into deep knowledge. It's the shock of poetic intuition which, after a brilliant debut, fades into the background only to reemerge later in the memory. Blowing out the birthday candles makes me a child again. The ice cream stand puts me back in my t-ball uniform celebrating after the big game. Visiting New Haven has me treading on ghosts of my old college days. The emotion is so powerful that it feels *necessary*.

Take, for instance, the Sign of the Cross that begins the Mass. The first time I lifted my hand, it traced out the frame of a new existence. I almost felt afraid and looked around after my hand dropped to see if anyone had caught me in the act. I was convinced my chest was blazing like dry straw and someone was bound to notice.

A thousand repetitions later, the Sign is a hasty action made while mentally composing a grocery list for later in the afternoon. We trace the shape of our salvation thoughtlessly. Carelessly. Until, one day just like any other day, I suddenly remember. The Sign of the Cross is a violently poetic act, the Christian sign of rebellion against a dehumanizing world. Through it, I steal a march on death because I have already died. I have a share in the Cross. My hand marks an epitaph, a preparation for a *pieta*.

I don't understand depression—why it afflicts some but not others or why some days are worse than others—but I'm familiar with its effects. Depression collapses the future to dust. It disorders time and closes the book so I never get to read the final sentence. So much time is squeezed out of me that the next tick of the clock precipitates doomsday.

Gerard Manley Hopkins calls this bitter, false ending carrion comfort. He was melancholic, too. Depression was a tempest that heaped his bruised bones to the ground. This carrion comfort makes me a visitor in my own life, cuts the anchor so I float away. I'm out there in the waves. Somewhere.

I suspect our current age is, generally speaking, melancholic. Its relationship to time is disordered. We fear death and pretend graveyards don't exist, ending up beholden to perpetual adolescence through avoidance, trapped in the conceit that time cannot progress if we refuse to allow it. Like a toddler playing a game, we place our hands over our eyes and pretend death no longer sees us. Careless to the future and learning nothing from the past, everything is in flux. Grasping tightly to the present moment, it is strangled in our hands.

Poetry is the solution. It exists outside of time but remains in intimate relation to it. Poetry is the creative shaping of some thing or some one into being, which is why poetic knowledge isn't an academic idea but, as a thing made, is known as movement, difficulty, and memory. As Wallace Stevens says, "Poetry is a pheasant disappearing in the brush."

Many of my parishioners have remarked that the Mass feels timeless. Past and future are joined to the fullness of the present moment.

When I make the Sign of the Cross, I lift my hand completely convinced that I am, as Rilke says, "much too alone in this world." By the time my hand moves up, down, left, and right, I've traveled infinite distance. No longer alone, I complete Rilke's prayer:

I want to unfold.
Nowhere I wish to stay crooked, bent;
for there I would be dishonest, untrue.
I want my conscience to be
true before you;
want to describe myself like a picture I observed
for a long time, one close up,
like a new word I learned and embraced,
like the everday jug,
like my mother's face,
like a ship that carried me along
through the deadliest storm.

With my hand, I trace a poem. With pierced palm, Christ makes the poem and I have a future.

✠ ✠ ✠

I often wonder if I feed into melancholy by trying to hold that which cannot be held. My flaws loom. Instead of facing them, I injure myself with the need to be in control. I clutch the flaws to batter them into submission only to flutter away on broken wing.

That's why it's odd that I waste so much time. I throw it away in heaps and piles like a spendthrift, staring at screens, apathy, alcohol, gossip, sin. I'm not a member of some productivity cult. I am not *driven*. In my mind, the problem isn't that I'm not productive enough. Quite the opposite, the problem is that, when I waste time, I'm not wasting it well enough. I'm wasting it all wrong.

I dream of perfecting the art of time-wasting. Currently, I'm practicing staring at the sky. Maybe the clouds will move or a bird dart past. I watch my children swim in the pond, yelping when the sunfish bite their legs. I help my toddler make oatmeal, read science fiction novels with pointlessly fantastical plots, and sit in the lightless church while the sanctuary lamp burns.

The only way I can figure out how to live my life is to waste it very carefully. After all, isn't prodigality the very expression of love? Isn't this what our Lord does on the Cross? Doesn't the Sower toss His seed wildly into the field? A musician voices a note into the air where it wavers and disappears. A mother releases her child from her bosom as a free creature who may never toddle back. A son remembers his prodigal father and returns to the fatted calf.

A child once asked Kurt Vonnegut how to write better. His advice was to write a poem and tear it up without showing it to anyone. It needed to be written for sheer love. Still, the universe is better for the poem having flickered into existence even for an instant.

Beauty seems unnecessary. When I tell people the Mass must be a poem, they comment that it's a nice idea, but then default to arguing for more functional purposes for the Mass. They say it must move our emotions, be relevant, cause sociopolitical change. We must "get something out of it." People cannot abide the notion that liturgy is wasteful. And further, that its wastefulness is necessary. We create elaborate, finely wrought liturgies as a way to tell God we love Him. Once the work is over, it's as if the poem is torn up.

The Mass is a slain flower. It's a poem or it is nothing.

If, like William Blake, I see God while sitting under an apple tree, but no one believes it when I say so, that doesn't mean it never happened. It doesn't mean the world didn't shift on its axis or a fruit didn't fall into the dirt like a tiny seed of eternity.

Through grace, I've accepted my battles with despair and let go of the need to control my spiritual progress. God isn't obliged to fix me. My flaws are so arbitrary, so sickly and sticky that I've wanted them eradicated immediately, but God allows certain limitations and sufferings for a reason. We come to the Mass as ourselves, honestly. If we don't, or won't, the Mass forces honesty upon us. Like any poem, it discloses self-knowledge, for good or ill. Unlike other poems, though, the disclosure is perfect. We see ourselves exactly as God sees us. We are gratuitous. Names traced in water. Seeds broken open in warm earth.

God doesn't need us. He does, however, love us. He binds bone and vein, gives bread and breath. He made you, His finest work of art.

As Hopkins breathlessly exults over the shipwreck of his life, "Thou mastering me / God!"

✠ ✠ ✠

I struggled with titling this book. I know that a book boldly proclaiming itself to be about poetics limits the number of you who pick it up to read (and thank you, intrepid friends, for picking it up to read). The relative unimportance of beauty is made clear when Catholics complain about the Mass. Less incense, they say. Look into our eyes and smile more. Wear plainer vestments. Sing more relevant music. Use the shortest Eucharistic Prayer. Don't use any fancy Latin.

Streamlined, efficient, bland prayers are symptomatic of priests and a Church that have forgotten themselves. Sometimes I'm asked where I learned to celebrate the Mass the way I do. Some people are under the impression that I'm making it all up because they've never seen a priest say Mass in a similar manner. It seems as though following the rubrics and contending for beauty is a rarity these days. My response? I learned from the Missal, from the Catholic Church. "This is our faith," I say.

So, for the title, I wanted an appealing, practical-minded phrase, something that sounded *vital*. I failed. Somehow, you managed to find your way here, a decision I hope you aren't regretting.

I wish poetics was trendier. Truth is widely preached from pulpits every Sunday, but truth isn't what parishes lack. It's beauty we've lost, not only in religion but the entirety of our lives. The effect of this lack was, for me, disastrous. My academic, arrogant mindset was drowning me, along with the idea that trying to live poetically was pretentious and artificial. I felt embarrassed because everyone called me a weirdo hipster aesthete. I was just trying to become myself.

The need to be useful is imprinted onto us from our earliest education. Happiness is supposedly functionality, a practical education for a good paying career. I ordered a daily subscription to the *The Wall Street Journal*. It didn't help. The search for control and productivity left me dissatisfied. I couldn't figure out why. I had no clue that there's real value in pausing to pick up a seashell or watching sunlight fall through a leaf, that those useless, whimsical actions voice God.

Even if it involves memory, a poetic act, as Gaston Bachelard says, "is not an echo of the past." Rather, it's a vibration seeking harmony with the soul. The poem has its own motives, carrying its own untamed spiritual dagger. A poem is its own kind of knowledge, called forth directly from the soul.

Poetry cannot be rationally explained. That's okay. Neither can the Mass or the invisible hand of divine grace. God's love for us is a baffling, unsolvable puzzle. Why doesn't He cut us rebellious children loose? In the same way, why not cut loose all the embarrassing, medieval ritual of the Church? Do the prayers need to be so intricate, so delicate, so foreign? Yes, they do. The Mass is God's language for *us*. Liturgy's purpose is feeding starving souls, but that purpose is quite enough. I'll wager, in fact, it's all we really need.

Made in the image of God, human beings already have one foot in another world. Beauty, poetry, and love are only extraneous if we forget about that world and define ourselves by material existence alone. Only if we're willing to go to war against our own selves.

We get so caught up in owning and using objects that we mistake the liturgy for another object. As an object, it's a failure. It holds no functional value. But it isn't an object. It's an invitation to discover your immortal soul.

I'd be thrilled if books about poetry were instant bestsellers. I'd be over the moon if parishes competed to create beautiful Masses that present all the diverse liturgical treasures of the Church, if we poured resources into the transcendent sacred. None of it is extra. All that beauty is for God. Burrowing down to the heart of existence, the Mass speaks of that which cannot be spoken in any other manner. As Paul Claudel says, there are no words of ours that God cannot transfigure. Perhaps, through the gift of beauty, Christ whispers, "And these feet are your feet, but look how I walk on the sea and / how I tread the sea's waters in triumph!"

✠ ✠ ✠

My interest in poetry began with desperation. I was helpless to address my depression in a healthy manner, let alone begin to name what I felt. But I would read a poem and feel understood. I wrote poems and felt heard. My emotions dropped their disguise.

Poetry is self-awareness, a new way of being. In a commentary on Psalm 32, St. Augustine writes, "Every one of us tries to discover how to sing to God ... so sing well, brothers!" It's ironic that this commentary is reproduced in the Daily Office for the feast of St. Cecilia who, although she's the patron of musicians, is famous for an act of silence. At her wedding, she declined to join the singing, choosing instead to sing to God in her heart. She sang well. She went to the source of the song, where it entered existence as pure love and returned love for love.

When we make the Mass beautiful, we return God's love to Him.

Poetry is a new way of being. "Towering up within itself," writes Martin Heidegger, "the work opens up a world and keeps it abidingly in force." As poem, the Mass creates a striving, a birth, through careful repetition of the words of institution but also in a more general way by voicing Christ, revealing sacred truth as an event. We're then able to make and recognize our Lord's presence in the wider world.

The Mass sets the context for our pilgrimage, our unity with Christ in His redemptive work. That which is hidden is unconcealed, and Christ is revealed to be all around, not only doing miracles *in* our world, but sustaining a miraculous world. Only poetry has this power, because what is hidden is not an intellectual concept but a world — the New Jerusalem, the Beatific Vision, union with Christ.

"Words cannot express the things that are sung by the heart," says Augustine. My boys and I war whoop as we rumble down secret forest trails. My toddler shrieks with glee as she jumps out of a closet to scare me. She makes bird calls through cupped hands to red cardinals perched in the winter-worn dogwoods. She fake-sneezes to alert me to her hiding place when I'm the seeker. It's all a new song. God delights in it. Love calling out to Love.

"Your heart must rejoice beyond words," says Augustine, "Soaring into an immensity of gladness, unrestrained by syllabic bonds. Sing to him with jubilation."

When I'm depressed, the beauty of the Mass comforts me. If you feel inadequate, broken, unlovable, sing the Mass. Sing it with your voice, in your heart — it doesn't matter. Sing the poem.

Emily Dickinson says poetry feels "as if the top of my head were taken off." Owen Barfield compares it to passing a coil of wire between the poles of a magnet to create electric bolts. As the language of movement, poetry creates spiritual progress. Each time the Mass is celebrated, the earth may as well physically quake.

The pilgrimage is daunting. I have far to travel, but that's good news. The future is pure potential. God has more to give.

The Mass is never tired. It's a celestial wheel of love tracing out a spiral of time as the stars silver into their cradles. Their sparks are consolation for a suffering soul, but the real grace is a white-hot coal that scalds the lips, the light blinding us to our aching knees, where we wiggle on the cracked plastic coverings of the kneelers, easing us out the door where, all along the sidewalk home, the bushes burn.

As a non-Catholic, I reinvented the wheel, frequently consulting the *Catechism of the Catholic Church*. It had the answers to every question. When I read it, everything made sense. I imported the theology and devotion of Catholicism into my life. As an Anglican pastor, I even considered myself in some way to be a Catholic priest, and English (not a Roman) Catholic, still a branch of the same tree. I was wrong, of course, but I was beginning to see the lines of the poem.

The inability to take in the whole strikes me as a cause of great unease. Maybe that's why we're constantly on the verge of giving up. We don't take time to contemplate God, or anything good and beautiful, really. We chase cheap pleasures and fill our schedules with activity. Worse, we become so addicted to the productivity trap that we import it to the Mass also. We jam liturgy with noisy activity and wonder why people abandon it so easily. Finding it too easy, they've found it unfulfilling.

A poem only reveals itself once we work from beginning to end. The work must be viewed whole, the end already present in the beginning.

I was stumbling through the dark because I hadn't yet read the end, hadn't circled back around and *lived* the poem. Although the Mass may appear to begin and end, it has no boundaries. It creates a collective memory of lasting duration in which we stretch our legs and move around. Think, for instance, of the invocation of the saints: "In communion with those whose memory we venerate." Suddenly, all the saints tumble out, reshaping the poem, the size of it, its characters. It's a great crowd gathered around the Eucharist, the One in whose memory we celebrate. It is our Lord in whom our memory finds its source. The Alpha and Omega.

Once I made it into the Church, I was given a new memory that shaped a coherent vision of the world. It wasn't as if I suddenly didn't have problems. I still suffer sadness and loneliness, self-doubt and self-consciousness, but knowing how the poem unfolds, its timeless beauty rooted in the Cross and Resurrection, I'm assured that this suffering is gathered up into the story of salvation. Perhaps this is the saving grace Hopkins felt when across his foundering deck shone an eternal beam: "That night, that year / Of now done darkness I wretch lay wrestling with (my God!) my God."

✠ ✠ ✠

The Mass is unrelentingly, unapologetically centered on Christ. Every action and word is His. In repetition, they grow in power. We come to worship, slightly different people than previously, with an expanded history and varying emotional states, but the Church remains, a spouse with the same stubborn love shutting up a fire in our bones.

The Mass is puzzling because it traces out the same pattern. Every day, I pray the Roman Canon, the prayer the Church has prayed for thousands of years. Every day I repeat the words of Christ. Every day the miracle happens. Some days I cry. Some days, considering the enormity of what I grasp in my very human, very frail fingers, I'm shockingly uninterested.

The vagary of emotions, the way we almost randomly attach ourselves to certain experiences and respond powerfully to novelty, is why so many mistakenly consider the Mass to be boring. We aren't good at pushing below the surface and prefer being spoon-fed with fast food and movies with car chases and explosions. We might even try making the Mass more emotional, but flash, modernity, and emotive elements only distract from the true excitement.

The Eucharist, like the sun, has risen once again.

Those who love the Mass know a secret. It's an ever-broadening act of love, an ever-widening circle of meaning, an ever-deepening encounter with the flickering fire of beauty that God has laid at our feet and placed in our hearts. Here, we find new footholds of love. You and I are always changing and developing, but our lives are firmly anchored to everlasting divine love. No matter what life throws our way, we are not lost. We are never lost.

The altar is cradle and grave, the place where life overlaps death, the lowest rung on a ladder to Heaven, the still place in the eye of the storm. Nothing is more exciting, nothing more relevant.

There are times after an evening Mass when I'm locking the doors at Epiphany and step out on the front porch for a minute as dusk settles over the city. Fireflies weave around on the field across the street in St. Louis air so humid and dense you can literally see it like fog, lingering incense over the grass. The fireflies are the last spots of light, the last signs of day as the dark closes over the roofline of the brick houses gathered along Arsenal Street. The final Mass of the day is over. There will be another one tomorrow morning, always another one. Always the precious devotions of the people who live and pray here. Christ always present with His people, day after day, world without end. For this I thank our Lord, who provides us with sustenance, His Body from which arises the sacrificial love that creates these moments.

These are the moments I sigh a contented sigh and am at peace with exactly who I am, depression and all.

✠ ✠ ✠

Many liturgical prayers end with the phrase, *Sicut erat in princípio, et nunc, et semper, et in saecula saeculorum.* That means, "As it was in the beginning, is now, and ever shall be, world without end." Amen.

By tradition, a *saeculum* is equal to the duration of time lived by the oldest person present. The current era, in other words, is defined by what remains within living memory. Once that oldest person goes to the grave, think of what is lost. Rebecca Solnit, in her book *Orwell's Roses*, opines, "It's sunset when the last person who fought in the Spanish Civil War or the last person who saw the last passenger pigeon is gone."

The poet Frank O'Hara considered suicide, but the thought that he wouldn't write any more poems stopped him. This isn't a whimsical story. He was literally rescued from depression and death by a poem—the one he hadn't written. He couldn't abide that any beauty would be lost.

For me, death was always before my eyes. I couldn't shake it. I saw no future. No reason I would ever be remembered.

Look again. *In saecula saeculorum.* The Mass holds us within the everlasting memory of the Holy Trinity. You'll never be forgotten.

✠ ✠ ✠

In researching this book, I read quite a few books on poetics. You should've seen me, snatching a minute here or there to read dense academic books by Paul Claudel and Jacques Maritain. I'd read a few pages, stare out the window, and turn back to the book only to encounter a toddler demanding I play dolls or allow her to ride on my back, "like a tiger." One day I was reading Rilke and a child quacked like a duck behind my chair. I jumped four feet high.

With six children, I read in fits and spurts. In any event, playing with dolls and kicking soccer balls is every bit as formative poetically as books are. I've benefited enormously from my time play-acting as a pony. Some of my best thoughts occur while buried under a pile of children.

It isn't a typical way to study. It fits me, though, because I have precious little academic rigor. It's a flaw, this lack of discipline. At best I'm a tourist in the field of poetics. I do, however, benefit from the overwhelming love that surrounds me, both in family life and in the Mass. Regardless of intellectual background, a simple homemaker possesses more wisdom about her home than a passing visitor, no matter how intelligent that visitor might be. The more love I give and receive, the greater my wonder grows, the more poetic my outlook becomes, and the closer I draw to God, the font of wisdom. The first requirement to live poetically is to love.

In academics, there's a pressing need to make up one's mind. Join a team, follow a philosophical school, expose the arguments of poseurs. Disagreements pop up even in poetics. For instance, Maritain says this in *Poetic Expression*,

> The poet is not, as Paul Claudel believes, a hierarch who "calls all things into being by giving each thing its inalienable and proper name." The poet would rather be a child who tames things by giving them the name of his loves, and who creates with them a paradise. They tell him their names in riddles, he enters into their games, blind-folded, he plays with them the game of life and death.

I want them both to be right and refuse to believe we can't iron out this little disagreement. Both writers have been influential on me and I cannot abide them fighting. I puzzled over it. In the end, I think they're both right, but we cannot solve everything through academic argument. We only behold the mystery and reverence it. We show reverence because we love.

Humility before mystery is everything. Parishioners have asked the meaning of certain words or gestures I use while celebrating the Mass. Sometimes I have a good answer. Other times I shrug. I have no clue. I simply follow the instructions. I imitate older priests and they in turn learned from older priests yet. I try to understand, but even if I can't, I know that poetic truth, including the unsolvable difficulty itself, is held in the arms of the mystery.

Christ is priest and sacrifice, God and man, first and last, Suffering King. It's too much. Enough to make me take off my shoes in awe and show up at Mass barefoot. Or remove them to throw across the room like a protesting toddler.

Here's an example. The Mystery of Faith is chanted directly after the consecration of the bread and wine. The priest genuflects and then sings the words. What you might not know is that, in older missals, the Mystery of Faith, the *Mysterium Fidei*, is buried right in the middle of the consecratory prayer over the chalice. It's shoved in there as a divine interruption, a dangling incompleteness that makes no grammatical sense. No one knows how it got there. This is why the phrase was moved when the missal was revised, but I cannot help but regret this change. There is much we don't understand and cannot reconcile. When this happens it's best to watch and wait.

I'm reminded of something Chesterton says about Charles Dickens: "He knows that loving the world is the same thing as fighting the world." A poet is hungry. A poet is thirsty. This is why beauty feels like a dull heartache, confronting us with the reality that beauty is a miracle violently pushed from eternity into time, bursting at the seams of everyday life and infusing every moment. Paradoxes abound, signs of the energy needed to pass beyond this world and into the next. It's all quite astounding.

Really, Maritain and Claudel don't need to agree. They're both pilgrims just like you and me. The Mass cannot be, shouldn't be, fully comprehensible. If I spend my days shuffling through the rooms of my house with a giggling toddler clutching onto my leg for dear life, well, that's progress too.

I don't need a literal burning bush before my eyes to make my imprudent demand. All my life I've wished God to tell me His name. In response, He speaks riddles.

✠ ✠ ✠

I've been trying to wrap my mind around why certain Masses bother me and leave me even more depressed. I've been told that, if the Eucharist is valid, the Mass is good regardless of how the priest and people behave. Or that participating in a casual, sloppy Mass which piles up liturgical abuses is a sharing in the suffering of Christ. I'm supposed to endure it, and if I choose to complain that's my problem.

This line of argument falls flat. We shouldn't be content to suffer abuses mildly or compromise with mediocrity. God deserves our best effort. He deserves beauty. Every single person deserves to experience His beauty in return. A Mass that doesn't lift its face to Heaven robs us of our daily bread and impoverishes our daily lives.

In youth, my sadness was complicated by the desire to live authentically while feeling incapable of it. I wanted beauty, meaning, and happiness, but had no clue how to achieve them. Everything I experienced—education, consumerism, religion, pop culture—fought against it. This is the tragedy of our modern era. We want love, acceptance, and purpose. We want to give ourselves to something greater than ourselves. Instead, we get roommates we never see, office work, and mindless entertainment. I remember searching out authenticity through painting and art, obsessive reading, messing around with Marxism, chasing girls, and getting involved in odd hipsterish pursuits. I brewed boutique coffee, shopped at thrift stores, went to trendy concerts in the Bowery, took up playing Go. It was all for naught. The desire for an authentic life cannot be fulfilled by this world.

Without the poetry of the Mass, I had nothing but increasingly frantic attempts to break out of the prison of modernity. My search for beauty met a dead end. Simone Weil explains, "Poetry can only have one source. This source is God. This poetry can only be religion."

There's no secret trick, no shortcut, no method by which we create meaning. A poem is miraculous because it draws from God's supernatural beauty. Our lives become beautiful only by participating in God's beauty. Forget this and you'll forget who you are. Perhaps I'd never even known who I was, and the more I insisted on defining my own existence, the depression only deepened.

We must forget ourselves in order to find ourselves. Poetry causes an unleaving, a forgetfulness that draws us into wider realities. The Mass destroys self-centeredness and brings us into God's household. We are made free through God's timeless, forgotten language, introduced to the romance of loving and being loved.

This, I think, is what bothers me about Masses that are neglectful of the poetic grandeur of what they really are. It isn't that I prefer different music, dislike change, or am a middle-aged curmudgeon. The problem is that, in changing the poetic shape of the Mass and focusing on our own desires, we force the Mass to speak an unnatural language unworthy of the worship of God.

This is how Masses become mediocre. A Mass is meant to express form and lyricism, the priest, altar boys, and parishioners each finding their proper place. The priest speaking gently and removing his personality to intercede on behalf of the whole community, facing God with the faithful in solidarity. The focus is clear. It's orderly but never performative. Several actions might take place at once; entire families are engaged; the music drifts from the choir loft and fills the space.

When we make the Mass a performance, with choir on display, lectors dramatically reading into microphones, and the priest smiling his best smile and saying good morning, the focus shifts onto ourselves. Thus, we are lost.

The poem cannot take life as anything other than a revelation. As a searching, desperate newcomer to the Mass, I wasn't intrigued by a show or impressed by an individual priest's personality. I met God and fell in love.

Teresa of Ávila says, "Without poetry, life would be unbearable." This, I know, is very much true of the Mass as well.

If poetry is a forgotten language, perhaps that's a feature, not a bug. A forgotten language for a people who must learn to forget themselves, who are taking on the likeness of Christ. The Mass must show us that image. How else are we to find it if not here?

When I drag myself to the altar with all my distractions, inadequacies, and melancholy, when I manage to forget myself for long enough to pray the Mass and meet our Lord, that's when I remember. Christ unties the knots pressing on my heart. My mind clears. The Host cracks like lightning, splitting clouds, parting veils, and a hand reforms me, the same hand that created Heaven and earth, and now, in His shape, I have room for a second life, timeless and wide.[4]

---

[4] To paraphrase Rainer Maria Rilke.

TEN
Beginning, Again

IT SEEMS TO me we are always struggling to be born. Some days, when I kiss the altar, I'm Mary adoring her slain Lord. Other days, I arrive as Judas in the night. Either way, He still insists on dying for me.

The altar is our Bethlehem, a cradle holding an infant already pressed into poem by a crown of thorns, a stone monument like a baptismal womb or a grave marker. Christ's suffering is love, and the love makes the poem. This is how that tiny baby surpasses His humility and reveals His true divine nature, and why St. John alludes to the fulfillment of glory through humility. The Word seems, at first glance, to be that and nothing more, an insignificant man. A fact. A note in the historical ledger to either be believed or disbelieved. Sure enough, He is a human man, but so much more.

Poetry suffers so deeply that it achieves the greatest freedom of all, the purest form of language. Circling round, descended from Heaven to earth and back again, Christ is a poetic revolution who swept away all my petty concerns. Because of Him, I'm not a passing fact. Neither are you. We're that and more.

Underneath all our words, our attempts to speak and be heard, to hear and understand, our infant babble and speechless silence—underneath those words is not a *what* but a *who*, and that who loves us very much. So much so that He pours the universal into the concrete, living and dying on this earth and continuing to live and die in the Eucharist. The transcendent squeezed into the particular. This is His work.

This means that you matter. The people who matter to you matter. Your concerns matter. The little patch of green garden below your front window with the pink peonies in spring, your parish church full of quirky, delightful people filling the pews, your wobbly, inattentive prayers at Mass, the work you do, the bonfire you built for the kids, the t-ball game you watched in the park. Your creativity is important, the love you give, those halting attempts to learn to play piano, your penchant for Saturday morning hikes, the steam from the cup of your morning coffee. You are the particular, a person unlike any other, and your life is meant to be a unique embodiment of the divine. This is your work.

This is what the Mass taught me. I matter. I am caught up in a great communion of saints, a member of a single Body of Christ, but I am still me and the body wouldn't be the same without me, for better or worse. God names us. He loves us. He pours His beauty into us.

Above all, this work is gathered up in the liturgy—a word that literally means a public work. Don't forget this sacred language of the Mass, the somewhat foreign, odd, countercultural worship of the Church. It's worth contending for. Some people think it's ridiculous, the reverence, awe, watered silk chasubles and old lace, chant flowing like waves to the shore, gently, covered in clouds of fragrant incense from which wavering flames light the lamp of home, and then the Host, the bells, the poetic mystery. This Mass that, by the hand of God, unmakes and makes. I think it saved me. It is saving all of us. I think it's everything.

About the Author

FORMERLY A PASTOR for the Anglican Church in North America, Fr. Michael Rennier was received into the Catholic Church in 2010 and ordained under the Pastoral Provision for former Anglican clergy. He now serves in the Archdiocese of St. Louis, where he lives with his wife and six children. Fr. Rennier is on the editorial board at *Dappled Things Magazine*, writes a weekly column for *Aleteia*, and contributes to his archdiocesan newspaper and *Adoremus Bulletin*.

Sophia Institute

Sophia Institute is a nonprofit institution that seeks to nurture the spiritual, moral, and cultural life of souls and to spread the gospel of Christ in conformity with the authentic teachings of the Roman Catholic Church.

Sophia Institute Press fulfills this mission by offering translations, reprints, and new publications that afford readers a rich source of the enduring wisdom of mankind.

Sophia Institute also operates the popular online resource CatholicExchange.com. *Catholic Exchange* provides world news from a Catholic perspective as well as daily devotionals and articles that will help readers to grow in holiness and live a life consistent with the teachings of the Church.

In 2013, Sophia Institute launched Sophia Institute for Teachers to renew and rebuild Catholic culture through service to Catholic education. With the goal of nurturing the spiritual, moral, and cultural life of souls, and an abiding respect for the role and work of teachers, we strive to provide materials and programs that are at once enlightening to the mind and ennobling to the heart; faithful and complete, as well as useful and practical.

Sophia Institute gratefully recognizes the Solidarity Association for preserving and encouraging the growth of our apostolate over the course of many years. Without their generous and timely support, this book would not be in your hands.

www.SophiaInstitute.com
www.CatholicExchange.com
www.SophiaInstituteforTeachers.org

Sophia Institute Press is a registered trademark of Sophia Institute.
Sophia Institute is a tax-exempt institution as defined by the
Internal Revenue Code, Section 501(c)(3). Tax ID 22-2548708.